The Voice Within

THE
VOICE WITHIN
Love and Virtue
in the Age
of the Spirit

HELEN M. LUKE

CROSSROAD · NEW YORK

1984
The Crossroad Publishing Company
370 Lexington Avenue, New York, NY 10017

Library of Congress Cataloging in Publication Data
Luke, Helen M., 1904-
   The voice within.
    1. Spirtual life—Addresses, essays, lectures.
I. Title.
BL624.L85 1984   291.4'4   84-17013
ISBN 0-8245-0659-6 (pbk.)

Acknowledgments
The chapter entitled "Suffering" first appeared in the February 1983 issue of *Parabola*.

Contents

Introduction

The *Voice Within* is a collection of essays and reflections written at various times over the past twenty years or so. They are attempts to define in words some of the thoughts and images that came from within and to relate them to the outer voices in our world. Part One was written during the 1960s when the winds of change brought much turmoil to the churches and to the religious orders. Part Two dates from both the sixties and the seventies and the essays were the bases for study in small discussion groups. Part Three consists of two tales as examples of the "voice within" speaking in images.

The "voice within" speaks to us from the unconscious (to use the terminology of C. G. Jung) and, whether or not we hear it consciously, it is an all-pervading influence in our lives. Those of us who attend to their dreams will certainly have experienced moments when an actual voice speaks with such authority that we know immediately that its words cannot be set aside, however little we may yet understand them, whereas other voices may make suggestions that are highly suspect. In the face of these it behooves us, as the First Epistle of John urged, to "question the spirits whether they be of God" (4:1).

Anyone who seeks for meaning in his inner life must therefore learn to listen with all the discrimination of which he or she is capable for that which he or she recognises, however dimly, as the ultimately single voice with a thousand names. It comes to us from the ground of our being and brings in a unique way to each individual an intuition of the unchanging oneness of life. It speaks through word or through image and the looking and the listening are ultimately one experience when we have ears to hear and eyes to see.

It is our task to "test the spirits," or voices, through the effort of expressing them, re-creating them, perhaps in an audible or visual form of our own, and certainly through the realization of their meaning in our actual lives. We are inspired and carried a long way by the "seers" who have gone before, by great poetry, art and music, and by the creative spirit of all whose lives have touched our own, but ultimately no one of us can hear the voice more than partially without his or her own unique re-creation, whatever its form, and quite irrespective of its merit or importance in the eyes of the many. All our efforts will seem inadequate: we fall again and again into mistakes, inertia or *hubris,* but it is the perseverance itself that will sharpen our hearing— not success or failure.

The word *voice* has a meaning in grammar defined by the *American Heritage Dictionary* as "a verb form indicating the relation between the subject and the action expressed by the verb" (active and passive voices). This is a beautiful hint about the meaning of the voice within. It is a voice that reveals to us the relationship between the subjective and objective truths of our lives. It brings into consciousness the acceptance of the human condition in which we must suffer the tension between active and passive, inner and outer realities, between all the opposites of life, and it leads us ultimately to an intuition of the whole in which subject and object are one.

Love and Virtue in the Age of the Spirit was carefully chosen to be the subtitle. It has often been said that in English we have only one word *love* with too many different meanings and that we need other words. Nevertheless, in all its connotations, whether it is describing pure lust or the most spiritual devotion, its universal use affirms the ultimate truth that the life-force of creation at the core of every human being, however blindly we may pervert or project it, is the divine spark of love that drives us to the search for our lost wholeness.

The word *virtue* is out of fashion these days. It has several definitions in the *American Heritage Dictionary,* the two main ones being, in part: (1) "The quality of moral excellence . . . and responsibility. . . ." and (2) "Conformity to standard morality or mores. . . .'' It is a fine old word, debased by its association with a narrow and unconscious conformity to what is "respectable." The original meaning of the latin *virtus* was manly strength; *vir,* of course, means man. We do not, however, have to think of it as an instance of male chauvinism. *Virtue* has always been used as an attribute of both sexes, implying the capacity of every member of the human race to take up the responsibility of an ethical attitude to life. The phrase "the Age of the Spirit" I have used to express the particular challenge of the era that is now dawning in our world. The past years have seen the ever-increasing expansion of the ego's powers over the external world of matter without relationship to the world of values within. This split has cost us the loss of meaning and the resultant horrors of disorientation and pointless violence, which could end in the destruction of the world. Nevertheless, in this extremity we are being driven to search again for meaning in our lives, and there are signs everywhere of the rebirth of this quest, which is in fact a longing for the experience of the voice of the spirit within.

This voice is speaking less and less in the language of collective institutions or through external rules of morality, and more and more in the individual soul. But our need for *virtus* and our responsibility for moral excellence is not thereby done away. C. G. Jung in a letter to Erich Neumann, written in 1957, spoke of what Neumann had called the New Ethic and said that it was not really a question of a *new* ethic but of "differentiated ethical reflections such as the question: How do I relate to the fact that I cannot escape sin?"[1] He quotes the uncanonical saying of Christ: "On the same day, seeing one working on the Sabbath, he said unto him, 'Man, if indeed thou knowest what thou doest, thou art blessed: but if thou knowest not, thou art cursed, and a transgressor of the law.'"[2] To know what we do—that is our hardest lifelong task.

Jung goes on to elaborate on our predicament—on the fact that we inevitably fall into sin. "I know that I do it, and know what I have done and know that all my life long I shall stand in the torment of this contradiction . . . but I shall make the best of a bad job, like the unjust steward who knowingly presented a false account. I shall do this not because I want to deceive myself, let alone the Lord, but so that I may not give public offense on account of the weakness of my brothers, and may preserve my moral attitude and some semblance of human dignity."[3] He then affirms that these reflections can only be valid for someone who is truly aware of his "shadow," because if anyone ignores his dark side or brushes aside his moral responsibilities he may be open to the dangers of compromise with evil.

Every fact, whether conscious or unconscious, is always paid for in this life "to the uttermost farthing." There is no individuation, as Jung said frequently, without fidelity to ethical values, and certainly no true realization of love without the *virtus* of the individual spirit.

> The living spirit grows and even outgrows its earlier forms of expression; . . . this living spirit is eternally renewed and pursues its goal in manifold and inconceivable ways throughout the history of mankind. Measured against it the names and forms which men have given it mean very little, they are only the changing leaves and blossoms on the stem of the eternal tree.[4]

Part One:

VOW AND DOCTRINE IN THE NEW AGE

1

The Spirit and the Law

We do not need the symbolic language of astrology to tell us that we are on the threshold of a new era. As the age of God the Son began with the coming of Christ to the Jewish world of the Father Jehovah, so in our day the age of the Son is giving birth to the age of the Spirit. The worship through two millennia of the incarnate God has indeed achieved its mission—and, as always, negatively as well as positively. Man has truly become godlike, with the magnificently subtle and powerful development of his intellect bringing an undreamed of control of nature, so that he even leaps up among the stars and has the power to destroy the entire world by touching a few switches. But with this power has grown another capacity of far greater importance—the capacity to think and feel individually, which was the deepest message of the Christ.

Christ's whole life was a breaking down of the collective laws and accepted beliefs that had been so essential to the age of the Father and were degenerating into sterile observance. If we are to enter into the "fullness of Christ" we must now find the courage to break with the laws whereby his teaching has been preserved for us and which now in their turn are becoming sterile. Only in this way can we listen to the new voice of the Spirit in the individual soul. This voice is speaking very clearly in the young who say, "I must be true to 'my thing,'" and every other value must go down before it. They are gloriously right, but alas, if this assertion of the validity of the Christ within remains

3

undiscriminated from the ego's inevitable bid to identify its lust for power, its concupiscent drives with the individual's unique "thing," then the result is not Christ but anti-Christ. Only the charisma of the Holy Spirit can save us from this disaster—the Spirit that is the love proceeding from Father and Son—that inner intuition of the Self that unites law and grace, responsibility and freedom, the "Great Symbol" whose birth transforms the "I want" of the ego and the "I ought" of morality into the liberty of conscious love.

It is an indisputable fact that the vows of the Church whereby the Christian faith has been affirmed are losing their sanctity, their binding quality, becoming, even as men swear to them, a form half-drained of meaning because there is in all of us nowadays, however unconscious of it we may be, a reservation. "Until death us do part." Even a devout Catholic, if he or she dared to look deep enough, would find that the buried reservation is there; he could get a divorce if worse came to worst; he could leave the Church without falling into Hell. Men and women go on taking the marriage vow in deep sincerity, but an increasing number speak the solemn words with an easy disregard of their full implications, and some with a cynical lightness without even the intention of permanent commitment.

So, also, even those who enter the monastic orders take their solemn vows of lifelong dedication with this unconscious reserve. Divorce has long been a commonplace, but the spectacle of thousands upon thousands of dedicated men and women seeking release from their religious vows is new. Twenty years ago it was a fairly rare thing for a "religious" to leave his or her order after making life vows, but today it is already a thing accepted, even by the devout, as calling for little comment. In the case of the baptismal vow, it has long been for many Protestants, and for semi-believers, a convention—often not much more than a social occasion. This trend is inevitable as the connection of the rite with its symbolic meaning grows increasingly weaker.

Here is the crux of the whole matter. The power and the beauty of all vows are derived from the *symbols* that gave them life. Every monk or nun in any age, having taken the great vows of poverty, chastity, and obedience, has pledged himself or herself to live his or her whole life as a visible symbol of those three interior states of consciousness without which *no* person, in any walk of life, can come to the realization of God and of wholeness as an individual. It is the same with the marriage vow. The symbol behind it is the Holy Marriage—the union of Heaven and Earth, of the two fundamental forces at the root of all life, the Yang and the Yin, the male who creates and the female who gives birth. All men and women taking the marriage vow are thereby promising to bear witness in their outer lives together to this inner vision of the final unity. The difference between a sacramental marriage (whether celebrated in church or out of it) and a liaison, or a mere social contract, is precisely this. In the latter there is a simple joining together of two people on one or more levels, while in the true marriage there is an ever-present third thing—the living symbol without which no meeting between man and woman has any ultimate meaning.

In the age of faith, the ego was still relatively undifferentiated, and men and women were not yet far removed from the primitive condition in which the material world and the numinosity of the unconscious were an undivided reality; it is therefore not surprising that the penalty for the broken religious vow was eternal damnation, that the heretic was burned at the stake, and that the penalty for adultery was death. To us it seems that these things were horribly cruel and barbarous customs and we congratulate ourselves on being more enlightened. We do well to reflect on the barbarities of this century, such as the pure evil of the Nazi creed, which is by no means dead in the so-called free world, before we feel superior. For the cruelties of the ancient laws were, given the premises of collective consciousness, at least based on a sense of meaning in the universe. When there was no clear discrimination between exterior and interior reality, it was a matter of course that the human beings who took these vows and broke them should be subject to the same consequences in the flesh as are inherent in the unbreakable logic of the archetypal world. The split between God and his creation, between Heaven and Earth, as is made plain in so many creation myths, means inevitably the coming of death; therefore the woman who is unfaithful to her man must die. The pride of Lucifer's deliberate disobedience brought upon him his fall into hell; and so a man's refusal to obey must mean hell for him. Indeed, the definition of Hell is just this—the refusal in full consciousness of obedience to the recognized voice of God.

These facts of the unconscious do not change; but the question that must be asked and answered over and over again in every age is, "How is man to recognize the voice of God?" For Christendom the answer through many hundreds of years was that the Church was ordained by Christ to interpret that voice for all men; and for the vast majority of men it was indeed true that *extra Ecclesiam nulla salus*—"Outside the Church there is no salvation." As collective consciousness approached adolescence, the Reformation emerged, and with it a growing respect for the freedom of individual answers. Nevertheless, as is usual in adolescence, the rebellion against the outworn interpretations brought with it a threat to the truths themselves. The revolt against dogmatism threatened the basic truth of dogma, the emergence from blind superstition created the tendency toward contempt for the living symbol itself, and religion began to disintegrate into a rigid code of morals.

From the Reformation to our own day the differentiation of ego consciousness from the unconscious has proceeded with great rapidity until the split has become so wide that only a totally new approach to the great question, "How are we to recognize the voice of God?" can save humankind from the terrible loss of meaning that is the price it pays for this one-sided development. Man can, indeed must in this age, seek *individually* his interpretation of the voice within. First Freud and then Jung were the great pioneers, and the "way of individuation" that Jung both lived and charted for us with such depth of poetic vision, is the same "way" that the dogmas of the Church define, interpreted anew for our age. The new approach, however, has brought with it a great danger. The outgrowing of all collective answers exposes men and women to the equal and opposite blindness of "individualism." Everywhere we see a woolly-minded tolerance, or else rebellion for its own sake breeding again its opposite—a complete disregard of the values of the individual and a new kind of total authority. However unconscious of it one may be, everyone's need is to find the totality—the wholeness—that is God. The more we are cut off from the symbolic life, through which alone we may approach and reconcile the opposites, the greater the danger of our projection of this reality onto totalitarianism of one kind or another. The total authority of the Church is replaced by the total authority of unbridled instinct and we have the spectacle of the grandeur of the free spirit of the individual reduced again to a conformity, this time devoid of all meaning.

In the midst of these growing dangers, it is alarming to see the failure of the Church to respond with vision and guidance. It will be said that all the churches are vibrating with new voices, and this is true; but what are they saying? Instead of reasserting the eternal values of the interior and the symbolic life in the individual, they appear to be joining in the flight from these truths which it is the whole function of a church to maintain. They seek to put in their place a well-meaning assertion of *relative* human values, social action, etc., as though these things could make up for the decline of worship. There are even those who openly advocate the "demythologizing" of religion, which means, of course, the destruction of the religious function itself.

The storm over Pope Paul VI's encyclical *Humanae vitae* on birth control is an example of how the whole point is missed— not only by the Pope himself and the hierarchy, striving pitifully to answer the great question in the old outgrown way, but by most of those who protest against this blindness. If the sanctity of the commitments that express the fundamentals of Christian faith (or of any faith in life and love as having meaning beyond the desires of the ego and the concepts of the intellect) is not to be lost and sink into a matter of social good intentions or meaningless license, then indeed it is time for a new assessment of their meaning and application to outer life. What is needed is not a loosening of the binding quality of these vows, but, on the contrary, a tremendous assertion of their validity and permanence, not as promises to be kept in a fixed and unchanging frame of reference in this world, but as absolutely binding *inwardly,* informing all the constantly changing circumstances of one's outer life with meaning. We can no longer disregard the split between the conscious and unconscious and cling to the illusion that by following the old rules we can still be protected from the dark things below and from the individual responsibility to find one's own way in which to be true to one's basic commitment.

What, for instance, could the Pope have said on the issue of birth control that would have resolved this dilemma without watering down the Church's age-old teaching and that would have challenged bewildered men and women to a new and deeper understanding of the meaning behind this ancient prohibition? It is an eternal truth that where there is an act of generation, it is a sin against all the values of life, divine, human, or natural, to take steps to ensure that no new life is born from that act. The meeting of male and female, of seed and egg, of divine and human, is quite meaningless if all possibility of creation is eliminated beforehand. Archetypally it is as though the Holy Spirit, as he descended into the womb of the Virgin, had said, "I have made sure that no child shall be born. All that will happen is that you will feel special." But when the Church, at the present stage of human growth, holds to this as meaning that no man or woman may have intercourse without intending a physical child, it is surely interpreting this truth of the inner world in so blind and cruel a fashion as to be totally *untrue* to the real meaning of the eternal law.

At the primitive stage of consciousness this literal interpretation was, of course, valid. In the final return to unity it would again be valid but unnecessary—matter and spirit being one thing. But we are cast out of Eden, and there are two levels of truth—the truth of fact and the truth of meaning. It is our task to look through the outer fact to the inner meaning, and we can experience their final unity only through living contact with image and symbol. All our problems come from confusion between these two levels of reality, from their unconscious identification on the one hand, or their complete separation on the other. Only after the long effort of discrimination can we make the leap beyond fact and meaning to the truth which simply "is."

Men and women whose love is expressed in the sexual act may be creating a new value between them in their relationship, each in his or her own inner world, which is in very truth a "child." The constant fear that a physical child may be born, rejected and unwanted in the moment of conception, adding perhaps an intolerable burden, may in fact destroy the creative meaning of the act on all levels but the physical. "Marriage," says the encyclical, "has two aspects, unitive and procreative," and it goes on to assert that the unitive function is permissible without the procreative only when there is some physical or medical reason for the prevention of birth. There is likewise no sin, it continues, in sexual intercourse when the time is carefully chosen to avoid the likelihood of conception.

This statement appears to be mere quibbling. Either there is no choice whatever—everything is divinely appointed and the processes of nature must never be interfered with or, if choice is allowed to the individual at all, it becomes his responsibility on all levels. There is no word in the encyclical of the real sin in this matter, which is the sin of intercourse without creation of *any* kind—sexual indulgence without love, without tenderness, without responsibility, from which no new and lovely thing can possibly be born except physically. The unitive and procreative aspects of marriage, of all sexual activity, can never be separated, and a reading of the encyclical in fact leaves one with the feeling that the church is exalting physical values far above the truths of heart and spirit. Instead, she could, if she would, proclaim the truth that every true meeting between the opposites *must* give birth or it is a fruitless mingling, the sin of destroying meaning. At the same time, she would assert the ultimate responsibility of every adult man and woman to decide whether or not the act of union shall include a child of the body—whether or not they are prepared and able to love and rear that child with true devotion. Arid prohibition would disappear and its place would be taken by a shining faith in the dignity and wisdom of men and women in their search for the divine birth.

2

The Marriage Vow

"I take thee . . . to have and to hold from this day forward, for better or worse, for richer or poorer, in sickness and in health, to love and to cherish, till death us do part . . . and thereto I plight thee my troth." There are few more lovely words in the English language. The man who speaks them with all his heart, standing in the holy place, is pledging himself to more than the personal marriage between himself and his beloved. She carries for him in that moment, consciously or unconsciously, the image of all womanhood—of that which nourishes and gives birth, not only to physical children but to all the values of true relatedness and to the tender understanding of the heart. To the woman in her turn, her man is the symbol, however obscurely felt, of the sword of the Spirit—of the clear shining of the Word in the darkness. So they take this most solemn vow to love this innermost beauty and cherish it, no matter what the cost, as long as life shall last. Many who have no use for the Church and its rituals will find themselves moved at a wedding as their unconscious responds to the deeply buried image. For the two before the altar are more in that moment than simply the "John" or "Mary" whom we know; they are the symbols of the marriage for which all men yearn in their hearts—the I-Thou meeting, the marriage of Heaven and Earth.

The fact of this commitment in a dimension far beyond their ego consciousness does not, of course, mean that their promise to each other in this world is in any way weakened or devalued.

On the contrary, they are now pledged to the daily attempt to live as truly as they are able the meaning of the symbol in all their dealings with each other. They have chosen a partner in their search with whom to bring forth children, both human and spiritual. There is no hope that they will be able "to love and to cherish" each other unless each is prepared to accept his or her own darkness and weakness and to strive for the "holy marriage" within, thus setting the other free to find his or her individual reality. If there is a continual growth of consciousness through the daily abrasions and delights, and through the hard work of maintaining contact with a sense of the symbolic, then indeed they will together grow into maturity of love. Those who do not marry are equally committed to find partners on their way if they are to know love, bringing the symbol to incarnation in all their relationships with others of whatever kind—with their friends, lovers, enemies, or casual acquaintances.

Married people, however, have made a particular choice, and I am not suggesting that they are not bound to stay with that choice in the face of even repeated failure, as long as there is even a small chance that by staying together they may grow into love. If we break vows for any other reason than out of obedience to a more compelling loyalty, then the situation from which we have tried to escape will simply repeat itself in another form. Nevertheless, for thousands of men and women who take the marriage vow in sincerity, the test of daily life through the years makes it plain that the choice they made was conditioned by projections, which, as they fade, leave exposed the fact that the two personalities are, or have become, destructive of each other; or perhaps their levels of consciousness are so far apart that their bond is the cause of their drifting further and further away from the true meaning of their vows. These thoughts, of course, have no validity for those couples who never had any motive in their mating except the satisfaction of their immediate desires and ambitions. For them the vow is in any case devoid of significance and whether they keep it conventionally or not is of no ultimate importance except insofar as children are affected.

Divorce does not always mean that a marriage has been a failure. There are some marriages in which, though both partners have been true to their vows, and have grown through the years into a more adult love, a time may yet come when unlived parts of their personalities are striving to become conscious. A situation may then arise in which it becomes obvious that if they remain together, these two, who basically love and will always love each other, will regress into sterility and bitterness if they do not have the courage to accept the suffering of parting. Their quest for wholeness may then demand that they ignore the outer laws of church and society in order to be true to the absolutely binding inner vow "to love and to cherish from this time forward." One does not have to be living with a person—or even to see him or her ever again—in order to love and cherish through everything. A conscious acknowledgment of failures, an unshaken devotion to the love that sets free, can turn a divorce into a thing of positive beauty, an experience through which a man or woman may bring out of the suffering a purer love to all future meetings. The divorce is then a sacrificial, not a destructive act, and the original marriage may remain in the deepest sense procreative to the end of life.

It will be said that the promise at the altar includes the words "and forsaking all others keep thee only unto her as long as ye both shall live." The essence of this vow is a commitment to the utmost loyalty and integrity of which a human being is capable. It is a statement that a man's physical actions are as much a symbol of the singleness of the holy marriage within as any other part of him. In our state of partial consciousness, however, it may and does come about that the man or woman chosen no longer carries the symbol for the partner in any way at all, so that all love, all creation, is dead between them. Surely then the greater loyalties lie in the conscious acceptance of failure and separation. Thus each is set free to seek once more the realization of inner singleness of heart through new experiences of relationship and sex, through a new marriage, perhaps. "Until death us do part." When the symbol is dead between two people, when there is no communication left except on the level of the ego swinging between the opposites, then, if they cling to the letter of the law, a horrible betrayal of the marriage vow results in the unconscious, where animus and anima struggle to destroy each other. Death has parted them in the most real sense of the word.

Yet the Church still clings to its undifferentiated attitude to these things, she refuses to her children the opportunity of growth through a second marriage, and clings to the rules without regard for individual truth. I read the other day of the simple and beautiful ritual of divorce in the Orkney Islands long ago before the coming of the courts of law. The couple who had decided to part had to go into a certain church together and then quietly go out of it, one by the north door and one by the south. That was all. It was surely the perfect symbol of a true divorce— a hint of its potentially holy character. The couple returns to the altar before which they made their vow as though to renew it in the moment of their parting. One does not stand before the altar in order to announce that one is deliberately about to commit a sin. That simple ritual is an image through which we can feel the humble acceptance of failure, respect for individual responsibility, and the seeking of a blessing on a new attempt.

One of the great arguments against recognizing divorce is always the damage that the broken home brings to a child. If it were possible to assess this kind of damage, it would almost certainly be found that the hurt that is done to a child through the unconscious, when he or she is forced to live with parents in whom love for each other has turned to bitterness, is far worse than that caused by a physical breach. However successful the parents may be at covering up the fight between them, the child will suffer the terrifying consequences through the unconscious and will often carry the unsolved conflicts of his father and mother all his life. Insofar as a divorce really means a new chance for the parents to learn to love and is not just a running away, it can be a great gift to a child. Outer-seeming which is not true to the inner condition is a deadly thing—far worse in its impact on others than forthright, passionate sin.

3

The Religious Vows of Poverty, Chastity, and Obedience

To all religious who have a sense of the interior life, the vows of poverty, chastity, and obedience mean far more than the renunciation of material possessions, celibacy and obedience to the rule and to their superiors. Nevertheless, as in the case of the marriage vow, few voices have yet been clearly heard within the Church, breaking through the present ferment of change, to proclaim the eternal meaning within every individual soul of these vows and the temporal and changing nature of all outer structures by which men and women seek to live them. The result of this silence is that large numbers of sincere people, aware of an increasing meaninglessness in the rules they have promised to follow, seek to restore life to the old kind of structure by tinkering with its forms. They change or abolish the habit; they try to form small groups within their order and undertake new kinds of work; they reduce the number of offices, alter timetables, demand the right to engage in social action, and so on. Others leave their communities altogether and among these, many perhaps carry unconscious guilt for the rest of their lives, in spite of the formal release that may be given to them.

The use of the phrase "release from *vows*" is in itself a revelation of the lack of discrimination in the Church between the deep commitment of the vows and the varying disciplines to which a man submits in his attempt to keep them. Surely there should be no talk at all about "release." Not only monks and nuns but no human beings anywhere are ever "released" from allegiance to these three commitments if they would come to the company of the Blessed. If a man has promised to follow the monastic way of life outwardly, he is pledged to seek and live the realities of poverty, chastity, and obedience, in the context of that way, through doubt and suffering, aridity and discouragement, for just so long as the symbol behind this way remains alive for him. The moment it is dead and he knows it without question, then *because* of his vows, not in spite of them, he must dare to break with the safe conformity of the known, the support of law and habit, and must seek a new symbolic life in which to devote himself to those deep commitments. The vows must now be lived more profoundly with less support and the new inner discipline will be far more difficult than the old.

There are certainly very many individuals among those who leave the orders and among those granting release who understand this. Indeed there are signs that large numbers of religious have seen this essential truth. Nevertheless, is it not time for a clear and unequivocal statement of these values by the authorities of the Church? So very many bewildered and less conscious souls, caught in half measures, driven to neurosis by guilt, would be supported and set free to find inner reality according to their capacity by such a positive call to turn their gaze from the letter to the spirit of their vows. Definite encouragement to leave, as an act of devotion, not of failure, is the need of those who obviously cling to the monastic way for infantile reasons that stifle for them any possibility of growth, any chance they may have of understanding the real meaning of their commitment.

The wind of the Spirit is blowing, sweeping away the old law, but many religious of goodwill are bound to the old by their sincere acceptance of the fact that they have made a vow that binds them to the structure itself. A wise mother superior said recently that if the Holy Spirit wishes to destroy the religious life as we know it, then so be it. If an old thing is destroyed, however, it may disappear in one of two ways—either by slow disintegration with the authorities fighting a losing battle, a way that brings meaningless suffering to who knows how many; or by a conscious sacrifice whereby the values of the old are transmuted and reborn on a new level of meaning.

In childhood rules are an absolute essential, even when misunderstood and resented. A child is in misery when there are no fixed boundaries and he is asked to make his own decisions too soon, as witness the very many unhappy "little adults" whose parents have no notion of the difference between discipline and repression. So it was entirely right in the childhood of our civilization that the vows of the interior life, consciously taken, should include the imposition of unbreakable rules for outer behavior. This is no longer tenable. A true resurrection may await the religious life if Christians can pass through the present adolescent stage of rebellion to the freedom of full individual responsibility. The meaning of poverty, chastity, and obedience in the Kingdom of Heaven which is within can no longer in our time be bound for life to an unbreakable outer rule of any kind whatsoever. Conversely, we cannot without disaster dispense with outer rules until the true meaning of the inner reality begins to dawn in us, until we are aware of that which we seek.

What, then, are those three great visions that are the foundation of the interior life? In all religions, east and west, they are the same. "Blessed are the poor in spirit, for theirs is the Kingdom of Heaven." "Blessed are the pure in heart for they shall see God." "Blessed are the meek for they shall inherit the earth."

Poverty

"Blessed are the poor in spirit, for theirs is the Kingdom of Heaven" (Matt. 5:3).

The "poverty" of the religious orders and communities, that is, the renunciation of all personal possessions, is a symbol before the world of that inner poverty of spirit that is the Way for every man and woman. The outer fact of possession or lack of material goods is beside the point. The poor man demanding his "rights" and the rich man clinging to his wealth are in like case. A vow whereby a man or woman renounces material possessions, and, incidentally, is relieved of the responsibility of earning a living, is not only meaningless but actively harmful the moment it loses its inner meaning—the moment it is clear that freedom from outer concerns has become an escape for any given individual, and therefore a hindrance to his or her quest for spiritual poverty. Such a person will then be hiding behind a religious habit, identifying ego with clothing, instead of wearing it with a humble consciousness of its beauty as a symbol.

The changing attitudes of religious toward the habit, particularly in the women's communities, are the clearest possible proof of the loss of a sense of the symbolic. For the habit was the image that declared to the world that the man or woman who wore it had renounced not only material possessions but the *claims of the ego to any kind of specialness.* This is why the habit used to be held in such reverence both by its wearers and by the world outside. It awoke in its beholder a response, an effect, whether positive or negative, springing from the unconscious desire in every man and woman for that very poverty of spirit whereby alone we possess the Kingdom of Heaven. To give up specialness is the very reverse of giving up uniqueness. Poverty of spirit is richness in the Spirit, which can be known only by the man who has found his unique individual meaning and accepted anonymity in the context of society.

The habit is now increasingly looked upon merely as an uncomfortable and impractical uniform, to be abolished or approximated to ordinary dress. If the numinous meaning has gone from it, of course there is no sense in maintaining it; the halfway measures, the rationalizations are the damaging thing. For we cannot go back. Once the manna has departed from something, we must let go of it; but unless it is a conscious sacrifice out of which the symbol is resurrected on another level, then the old imagery will simply disappear into the unconscious and turn negative. The symbolism of the habit is losing its numinosity because the collective way of institutional religion is no longer for most people anything but a social activity—often of great value on that level but unconnected with the interior religious life of the soul. It cannot be too often repeated that, as Jung said, it is impossible to replace a symbolic with a rational truth. Those who see the habit as a uniform to be abandoned are moved by their urge toward outer individual differentiation, but, if at the same time they lose contact with the numinous image altogether, then the change defeats its end. It is an illuminating fact that the conservative, contemplative orders are losing fewer of their numbers than the progressive, active communities.

Meister Eckhart defines poverty as that state of being in which a man is wholly detached from "things," and to the extent that he empties himself, just so much does God enter into him and fill his emptiness. In our own time Jung has defined the same reality as that wholeness that a man may know when the ego, through experience of the great symbols in the unconscious, is purged of all demand and concupiscence and is replaced at the center of the psyche by consciousness of the Self in which the opposites unite. Those religious who feel that they are called to activity in the world are still bound by their vow to the immensely difficult task of holding inwardly, in the midst of all action, to the poverty of spirit in which there can be no demand for results of whatever kind, no matter how 'good' they may deem their goals. It is obvious that, as Jung said, only the transcendent and numinous symbol in which the two realities of matter and spirit, of conscious and unconscious are united in a single image can take a man "beyond himself and beyond his entanglement in the ego" to the resolution of this paradox, to the blessedness of the poor in spirit.

Chastity

"Blessed are the pure in heart, for they shall see God" (Matt. 5:8).

This is the reality of the vow of chastity. The renunciation of the instinctive life breeds dark and ugly things as soon as it loses its symbolic meaning and becomes mere evasion. If the instinctual urges have been experienced without repression, emotionally and physically, and the agony of no fulfillment of those levels consciously endured, then to those few who are capable of this way will come a great transformation of love through suffering. They will create and give birth in the realm of the spirit where there is no marrying or giving in marriage. But as a way of life unbreakably imposed from without on adolescent souls who so often are not able to realize the evasive motives underlying the promises they made in good faith, it may lead over the years to an impurity of heart more dangerous than the open concupiscence of the prostitute.

Purity of heart has nothing whatsoever to do with sexual intercourse as such; it is a matter of the quality of love. There is plenty of adultery between very respectable married couples,

for every mating is adulterous where there is no love and no creation. The purity of heart that brings the vision of God, like poverty of spirit, will come to us only when our love, our desire is
free from every *demand* for fruition.

We must be clear about the distinction between the demand
and the desire itself, for these two things are very generally confused, with deadly effect. It is essential that we allow our desires
absolute freedom if ever we are to be freed from unconscious demand. I cannot do better than quote here from Max Plowman's
book *Introduction to the Study of Blake,* in which he comments
on one of Blake's poems. There are two verses in the poem, one
of which begins, "Love seeketh not itself to please," and the second, "Love seeketh only self to please." Max Plowman writes:

> Here are contraries that are true and must remain coexistent. . . .
> Without self-pleasing there can be no love. . . . Invertebrate sen-
> timental self-negation is the destiny of those who think love can
> be comprehended by the love that seeketh not itself to please. . . .
> Self-assertion is essential to individuality, and until we have
> achieved individuality through self-assertion, imagination cannot
> function. Love without desire is sterile; but love is redeemed from
> greed by imagination. That is the miracle.[1]

The word *imagination* is, of course, used in Blake's sense. For
Blake it meant the only power in man through which he might
come to the vision of God, the one way out of absorption in the
ego; and when he spoke of the life of the imagination he meant
exactly the same thing as Jung meant by the symbolic life.

We may come, then, to the love that is pure only through setting free the imagination in the world of symbol, and by
rejecting nothing of ourselves, dark or light. The way is over-
whelmingly hard and beset with dangers, for imagination can
very easily degenerate into daydreaming fantasy if it is undisciplined. No wonder, then, that there are rules to protect and help
us on the road; without them we should have no hope of
growth. But it is fatally easy for us to turn these rules into ends in
themselves, and the churches, whose whole vocation it is to protect us against just this betrayal, are too often the worst offend-
ers of all.

True celibacy, then, is not the outer state of remaining
unmarried; it is the inner condition that every man and woman,

married or unmarried, must seek if he or she is to "see God." It is the state of being whole, one-in-himself, so that he no longer seeks unconscious parts of himself in his relationships, whether with wife, friends, or enemies. Then he may come at the last to awareness of the marriage of Heaven and Earth that is God incarnate. For this reason the Roman Catholic priest is bound to celibacy, for he is symbolically the representative of Christ.

The ego in our time is so far from the unconscious, the onesided development is so powerful, that the imposition of a rule from without easily becomes a positive incitement to the priest either to identify his ego with his symbolic function or else to live his life comfortably in two rationalized compartments, and this amounts to a real betrayal of his vow. The priest in all of us is forever celibate, but the ego struggling along the way must pass through the fullest experience of personal relationship on all levels, physical, emotional, and spiritual, before it can find the purity of heart that is the vision of God. If we are to avoid both identification and compartment living, it is again clear that only the experience that comes through the uniting symbol can save us. This is the profound meaning carried by the Mass, and by all the sacraments, to those for whom they retain their numinous power.

Obedience

"Blessed are the meek for they shall inherit the earth" (Matt. 5:5).

The third vow of obedience is a commitment to total response at whatever cost to the voice of the Holy Spirit within. The enormous difficulty of recognizing "the still small voice," as we listen to the confused clamor of voices in the psyche, in no way excuses in any adult soul the comfortable acceptance of an unchanging lifelong substitute for the dangers of the individual search.

The word *meek* has nowadays an almost entirely pejorative meaning. Meekness has come to mean a tame kind of submission, and the nineteenth-century image of a "gentle Jesus meek and mild" is about as far away as one could get from what Christ must have meant when he said, "Blessed are the meek." Ronald Knox uses the word *patient* in his translation, and that is nearer the mark in our ears. A patient man is one who suffers without protest but *not* submissively. He consciously *chooses* obedience. The kind of obedience that submits without discrimination, out of fear or weakness, certainly "inherits" nothing; but that rare quality of unconditional obedience, each man or woman to his or her own deepest vision of truth, does inherit the earth, for nothing can shake the one who has it out of the calm which is born of a fundamental acceptance of all the phenomena of existence. This is not at all the same thing as fatalism or a passive state of noninvolvement. On the contrary, such a man will be profoundly involved in all the changes and chances of his life, content to live with his doubts, to risk mistakes and failure as wholeheartedly as he embraces his certainties.

The question is immediately asked, "How can a man know that his supposed vision of truth is in fact anything but a subjective delusion?" The answer is that of course he cannot know, but that is not the point. There is an unconscious assumption in most people that "subjective" and "deluded" are synonymous, whereas a subjective reality is every bit as true as a so-called objective fact. The vital discrimination is rather between the different levels of our desires. We betray our most real intuitions of truth by running after superficial opinions or longing. Nevertheless, the one necessity is that we be wholehearted in our obedience on *whatever* level: "Unless devotion is given to the thing which must prove false in the end, that which is true in the end cannot enter."[2]

Even Christ himself could not answer Pilate's question, "What is truth?" The only answer to that question was Christ himself. For this cause, he said, was he born . . . that he might bear witness to the truth that was in him. For this cause is every human being born—not to live out his or her life in blind conformity to this code or that but to suffer unto death for his or her own truth. To the discovery of this truth beyond both the desires of the ego and of intellectual concepts, everyone must bring the devotion of a whole heart and mind. I quote Max Plowman again, writing of the way to this discovery.

> At Pilate's historic moment the embodiment of truth stood before the embodiment of reason, and the challenge to truth was merely that of making itself explicable. This the truth failed to do with

consequences that turned the world upside down. Never again
has it been possible for a reasonable being to suppose that truth
can be encompassed by facts. . . . But every man, just insofar as
he is not a poet (using that word in its widest and truest sense) is a
descendant of Pilate, for truth of some kind man must have, and if
it is not the truth of poetry, then it will be the truth according to
law. . . . Poetry is not the vehicle of sound common sense, but is
a means of creating images, which, like the prism, ray out innu-
merable aspects of truth. . . . Our perception of truth is not dependent upon fact but upon intensity of imagination.[3]

It should not be assumed from this that intensity of imagination does away with facts. No indeed! True imagination is born
only out of the clearest possible discrimination of facts exactly
as they are, and the penetration through them to the symbol beyond them. This is why the man or woman who is obedient to
his or her imaginative vision inherits the *earth*. The down-to-
earth facts of everyday life are filled with meaning, and transformed by the image, they too become truth. Blake said of
himself, "I question not my corporeal eye, any more than I
would question a window concerning a sight. I look through it,
not with it."[4]

People laugh nowadays at the story of St. Teresa telling her
nuns that their vow meant unquestioning obedience even if a superior told them to go and plant a cabbage upside down. In our
enlightened times such supine obedience would be idiotic. But
the story has a beautiful symbolic truth. St. Teresa is in fact saying that the essence of obedience is imaginative, and that it has
no meaning whatever if it is merely a matter of following rational judgment. The man or woman who has entered a religious
order and promised to obey its rule out of an intense imaginative
experience of the truth it symbolizes will not be troubled by the
minutiae of that way of life, or by the often mistaken and meaningless interpretations of the rule on which superiors may insist.
He is obedient to his inner vision, and the way of his order with
all its faults may remain for him to the end of his life the outer
form through which the symbol becomes incarnate. But the moment the form becomes for him an empty conformity cut off
from the symbol—the moment his life regresses into a matter of
good works only and obedience to facts alone instead of truth,
then he is no longer among the meek who inherit the earth; he

becomes a tame cipher dominated by the "letter which killeth." The window has become opaque.

So it is for all of us, accepting this or that discipline, whether of work or relationship. To run from one opaque window to the next because its shape or color is different and pleases us better is quite pointless. The saint or sage, the great poet, can see through all windows, but he, too, has sought and found, through many choices and changes, that way of life through which the light pours for him most clearly, so that at the last he becomes himself a clear window for others. We see "through a glass darkly," as St. Paul says, but always *through* it if we would know truth.

When the chosen way of life has become something that obscures the living image, then, if a person begins to see the light shining through another window, he or she not only may, but *must* break every law, even the laws of the outer Church, in order to be true to the solemn and binding vow of lifelong obedience. The Church through her priests has only one unchanging function—to keep alive the numinous image behind every fact and every law, so that our choices may be made in obedience to the symbolic truth of the moment and not to the thousand and one conformities that are its substitute.

The simple people of goodwill, of whom there are so many in the religious communities, are in great need of this kind of positive help from their priests. They need to be freed from guilt and helped to the knowledge that there is no sin involved if they have found the rule to be something that stifles their growth, but equally that there is no substitute to be found simply by plunging into all sorts of other activities. It is a matter of putting the emphasis where it belongs—on the inner commitment. As Thomas Merton once said, even one monk or nun in a community who is there for the wrong reasons, and whose personality is stifled, will inject poison into the life of the whole. If this attitude resulted in the emptying of the monasteries and convents in a wholesale manner, what of that? The Spirit is not served by large numbers of people conforming to a rule but by the intensity of imaginative devotion in individual men and women, and society itself can be transformed by this kind of obedience alone. All other panaceas or crusades simply turn into their opposites.

4

The Mystery Within

Through the centuries most churchmen have taught that the mystical wisdom of Christianity is something for the very few. For hermits and contemplatives it was all very well, but the ordinary man had to avoid so dangerous a thing and hold safely to the outer rules of worship and conduct; and so, not only among scientists, but actually among professed Christians, the very word *mysticism* took on a negative meaning. Yet in our time, nothing can be a true answer to our need except the recognition that all humanity is called to the quest for the *mysterium tremendum* within. For many the way still lies through unconscious devotion to a collective symbol, but for an ever-increasing number nothing will serve but a conscious individual search for the mystery.

Nothing could be clearer than that the young of today have no more use for the collective following of rules, and that, consciously or unconsciously, they are desperately searching for the meaning of life through their own experience, through direct contact with the unconscious, with the living image. Speaking in tongues, the cult of Eastern mysticism, encounter groups, LSD, and the like are all symptoms of this search. But often these things result simply in a dangerous or pointless release of unconscious contents that the individual has no notion how to assimilate. The "establishment" has failed in this matter, and so the young seek to tear everything down and often do not know how to build anew. The danger can be very great, for the unconscious can swallow as well as nourish, and the Spirit from within, seized upon by the immature ego, becomes a demon overthrowing all human values. When men and women take these short cuts to the inner vision, the majority mistake emotional reactions for true experience, and gradually, for many, the responsibilities and hard work of ordinary life fade and seem humdrum and unimportant. Then indeed, the end is a descent from the superhuman to the subhuman.

It is not surprising that the way of the East appeals to many who, realizing their danger, seek new disciplines of an inner kind; but the Westerner who goes this way is exposed to another threat. With his highly differentiated ego he strives upward in meditation so that the split between conscious and unconscious becomes greater and wider, and he loses contact with his shadow and the values of humanity; or else, as in the case of Zen, true freedom is confused with the immediate satisfaction of desire. Great wisdom the East can teach us, but to copy the way of another culture is as unreal as any other kind of imitation. It is from within our own tradition that the new way must be born.

Eight hundred years ago a Christian mystic foresaw the essential spirit of the age that is now dawning. The Abbot Joachim de Fiore was the first to say that the age of the Son (New Testament) would be followed by the age of the Spirit. In that age, he said, there would be no more need for the hierarchy of the Church, for all men would then be contemplatives. He imagined it as a millennium in which every individual would have achieved the freedom of the Spirit that needs no law, but his vision was entirely accurate as to the meaning of our age. If their lives are not to dissolve into the meaningless, individuals in ever-increasing numbers will be forced by the breakdown of laws and by the rationalization of collective myth to seek, each within himself or herself, the contemplative vision.

Young Catholics who remain deeply faithful to the truth that they know to be alive at the heart of the Church try to restore meaning to their religion by such things as the alteration of ritual—whereupon, of course, it ceases to be ritual, the essence of which lies in unchanging, time-hallowed words and forms. A ritual is *born* from the unconscious and will certainly not be revivified by deliberate turning of poetry into prose, often bad prose at that, which is too often the result of these changes. In the attempt to make the great poetry of the Mass "intelligible" to all, the power of the old imagery is lost and replaced by something that, though it may be very fine and full of meaning on its own level, is simply not religion, and therefore no answer to the overwhelming need of the psyche for the *mysterium* within.

The young throw out the traditional words and rituals because of their yearning for individual spontaneity of feeling, speech, and action, and for community based on personal relationship instead of conventional structures. The taking of the Mass into peoples' homes is a beautiful expression of the "bringing home" to the individual of the inner mystery, but too often it may result in the banishment of *all* mystery. The silence and "secrecy" and the beauty of vestment and gesture in the old rite were an evocation of the sense of the numinous. The Mass is a drama, a dance of images, and in the old ceremonies the emphasis was on *looking*—for, as the mystics have always known, we become that which we look at, not that which we think about. The new experiments in the liturgy will stand or fall by their power to give life to the images in the unconscious and not by any appeal to conscious understanding. This is not to decry the value of conscious understanding—far from it. It is essential that we think—each one with all the clarity of which he or she is capable, but not *while* we are looking at the image, for the analyzing intellect will immediately destroy the numinosity. The whole point of a symbol is that it is an entirely different thing from an allegorical metaphor. It takes us immediately into the region beyond the definitions of the thinking mind.

The hierarchy of the Church has not yet made any attempt to interpret clearly for the faithful that for which they truly search and of which the changes in the Mass are the outer symptoms. Meaning, it would seem, is to be restored to the churches by banishing the inner silence—in which alone the voice of God may be heard, and by turning the attention more and more exclusively to action and good works. The new Masses reflect this attitude. It is now rare indeed to find anywhere an almost silent, contemplative Mass in the quiet of the early morning. One almost feels that no one can stand a moment of silence. Sermons have been introduced into all of them, and the involvement of the people has shifted from inner intensity to outer speech and action. Yet our need is precisely the opposite in this age of appalling secular busyness and collective thinking. The sense of the numinous, then, in Christian ritual is fast dying, and while we grieve at the passing of so much beauty, it is a fact to be accepted and understood in its positive meaning, for in an accepted death lies the seed of birth.

The Church of Christ has preserved through two thousand years the message of God incarnate. It has also rightly protected men in their weakness from the full impact of that message, as Dostoyevsky's Grand Inquisitor so clearly saw. The vast majority have been too weak to bear it alone. The ego, paradoxically, has to grow immensely strong before a man, alone and unprotected, can challenge its leading role. In the past men found salvation from the devouring greed of the ego by obedience to the wisdom of the Church and by response to the great symbols preserved in her rituals. It will be said that there is still a great majority who need this protection, and this is surely true. The Church must still fulfil her ancient task, but the help and guidance needed is of a different kind. The old language, the old emphasis, is becoming useless not only to the stronger souls but to the many. To bolster it up with a "social gospel" or a changing liturgy is like building a wall of sand to stop a flood.

The Church is ordained not to give specific answers on external issues, but to listen to the voice of the Holy Spirit and to interpret it with humility for all those individuals whose imaginative consciousness is not yet strong enough to enable them to find their own symbolic life. But of course an institution is incapable of listening to anything—only an individual can do that. If all those "chosen" ones from the Pope downward who choose a religious vocation were to listen individually to that voice like a breath of wind within, resolutely refusing to be distracted by any of the interpretations of the past, they would hear again the pure essence of the Faith in this new age of the Spirit. Then indeed the Church in her great wisdom and with all her symbolic power might speak to her children the *positive* truth of that urge to overthrow all authority, all discipline, all checks on the individual. She might say, "Yes, you are right in what you seek. This is the true voice of the Spirit. No outer law, no conformity of any kind can bring you to the meaning of life, to the vision of God. But if you have grown to this point, then the form and the discipline and the moral laws against which you rebel outwardly must be found inwardly, and the challenge of this quest is a great and exciting thing, far more exciting than an easy grabbing at 'experience' through the short cuts of drugs and indiscriminate sexual indulgence. It is a quest of the individual imagination, which is both contemplative thought and active love, whereby man finds in and beyond the fact the symbol that gives it reality."

Jung wrote:

> By becoming conscious the individual is threatened more and more with isolation, which is nevertheless the *sine qua non* of conscious differentiation. The greater this threat, the more it is compensated by the production of collective and archetypal symbols that are common to all men and women. This fact is expressed in a general way by the religions, where the relationship of the individual to God or the gods ensures that the vital link with the regulating images and instinctual powers of the unconscious is not broken. Naturally this is true only so long as they have not lost their numinosity; that is, their thrilling power. Once this loss has occurred, it can never be replaced by anything rational.[1]

As has already been said, it appears that the Church and the religious orders are doing just this—trying to compensate for the loss of the numinous with all kinds of rationalizations, instead of proclaiming the profoundly moving and thrilling truth that the Holy Spirit no longer speaks through outer structures and rules but in the living imagery arising from the unconscious "poet" in every individual man and woman. "The Spirit bloweth where it listeth and no man knoweth whence it cometh or whither it goeth" (John 3:8).

William Blake, two centuries ago, misunderstood by virtually all his contemporaries, dared to speak and to live this same truth. For him, as for Jung, the establishment of individual identity was the whole meaning of creation, and, as Plowman wrote:

> Whatever acted in opposition to that fundamental purpose was for him Satanic. . . . With the advent of Jesus man came to full consciousness and this consciousness required of him the abrogation of the old law and imposed on him the new law, the law of imaginative understanding.[2]

The Church that purports to interpret this reality must abrogate the old law over and over again and hold to the inner truth of the

Imagination (in Blake's sense)—the truth of the symbol in its ever-changing forms—hold to it even unto death. For the Church is the Body of Christ, and sooner or later the Body of Christ is crucified that it may rise again on a new level of being—in a new dimension. Then indeed another day of Pentecost may dawn. If the Church itself should disappear as an institution wielding outer authority because it dared to give to the individual complete freedom to seek his or her own way to live the mystery, then perhaps we should see a Resurrection beyond our hope, in which the Church of Christ—the Community of the "faithful"—would regain its true meaning as guardian of the interior sacramental life. In this age it will remain a guide to the many only through the individual vision of those of its ministers who have heard and followed the voice of the Spirit, which is beyond the law. The Body of Christ, crucified anew, may come again to the necessity of saying, "It is expedient for you that I go away. For if I go not away the Holy Spirit will not come unto you" (John 16:7).

Part Two

LOVE AND VIRTUE IN THE AGE OF THE SPIRIT

5

Courtesy and an Interior Hierarchy of Values

L et us begin by looking at the origin of the word and concept of *courtesy*. It was the standard of behavior demanded at the court of a king, the outward sign of the true aristocrat. The courteous knight of King Arthur's court, for instance, had to practice an unfailing gentleness and forbearance toward women; he had to be always true to his word at no matter what the cost, and he had to be ready to meet any danger arising from his task of protecting the weak and oppressed; he had to show mercy to the defeated and be devoted to the principle of "fair play."

All these qualities, though they have remained to this day as the hallmark of the true gentleman, have also degenerated, as do all collective ideals, into a rigid outer code of manners, and so courtesy has often become identified with mere politeness and conformity with the collectively "right" way to behave in given circumstances. True courtesy, however, is a kind of behavior that expresses a quality of the soul, an essential attitude of the whole person, and it is not by chance that the word takes us back to the court of a king; for, no matter if every king should disappear from the earth, the psyche remains, as Jung has said, aristocratic in its fundamental nature. In our dreams, as in fairy story and legend, it is the image of the king that carries the symbol of the ruling value, the ultimate authority beyond the law. Aristocracy means government by the "best," the most noble, and in the mature psyche it means the preeminence of the objective, impersonal values over the little personal demands of the ego. So the royal quality, the aristocratic principle, is that which brings courtesy, is that which annihilates at once all feeling of superiority or inferiority between person and person. Only a true inner hierarchy of values can bring true equality of persons; also, this equality—another paradox—can only exist where there is accurate discrimination of *factual* differences of ability and knowledge. In the counterfeit gentleman, high birth and breeding, or any outstanding quality, become not merely superior in their proper sphere, in their factual aspect, but are believed to constitute a superiority as person, and no degree of polished manners or correct behavior can turn that man into a real gentleman, a courteous person.

How do we distinguish courtesy in a man from mere politeness? We may start by translating the knightly code into our terms. First, the gentleness and forbearance toward women would be, in our language, an unfailing sensitivity to the claims of feeling value. Secondly, the knight's fidelity to his word implies for us a searching honesty with ourselves of which is born both trust and trustworthiness. Protection of the weak is the quality of acceptance and respect for the failures and inferiorities we meet within ourselves as well as in others, and the willingness to expose ourselves to any threat or to any labor rather than take refuge in contempt or repression or unawareness. Mercy to the defeated is that essential element of courtesy, the absence of personal resentment when wronged—again it is respect for every human being no matter how hostile he or she may be. There is a most rare and beautiful example of this in Julia de Beausobre's account of her terrible experiences when she was a prisoner in Communist Russia.[1] She tells the usual story of the attempt to break down her human dignity, and says that one thing alone was finally left to her—the intense determination not to allow her tormentors to succeed, because, if she yielded, she would commit a terrible sin *against the questioners* themselves, monsters as they appeared. In other words, her simple, universal, unshakable courtesy kept her related to the human persons hidden under the inhuman cruelties of her tormentors, and so both saved her own integrity and released them from a small portion of their guilt.

The final knightly quality, devotion to "fair play," is emphatically not the whining cry so often heard, "That's not fair—life is unfair to me!" It is rather devotion to the quest for freedom to be oneself, to make one's own choices, however mistaken, and the refusal to weight the scales in any conflict by using weapons that the opponent does not possess. For instance, a man may defeat another in argument by a parade of specialized knowledge or wit designed to make his opponent feel his inferiority or ignorance. A knight would throw away his sword if his enemy did not have one.

All these things are contained in that little word *courtesy,* and yet it is an immediately recognizable quality, and there is no need to know much about a man or woman to sense its presence or absence. A courteous person will always make everyone around him feel at his best and most alive. No matter how superior his knowledge, his breeding, and so on, he will bring to his meeting with another person an absolutely genuine interest, respect, and concern for that person; and above all, he will give him his whole *attention* without curiosity or demand, and so immediately communicate to the other a freedom and sureness of which, perhaps, he did not know himself to be capable.

A description of two actual people may well illustrate the difference between courtesy and politeness. Both these men were of superlative intellect and at the top of their particular fields and both were brilliant talkers. One of them, even in a group, immediately communicated, even to the youngest and most insecure, a sense of being appreciated for himself, not for his abilities or his contributions to the conversation, and all self-consciousness vanished. The other was a man whose superficial manners were impeccable, and whose taste was exquisite, but in his presence anyone whom he did not consider his equal felt devalued, awkwardly childish, and insignificant. His contempt or boredom was communicated without an impolite word being spoken. Another quality of this man was that he held all the ideas of a kind of chivalry. He was always on the side of the underdog, and passionate in support of the cause of justice and equality for all. He was kind and generous if anyone was in big trouble, but without, as it were, ever seeing the person in a true sense. Therefore, his giving was discourteous.

It is obvious that courtesy is not to be equated with "kindness" in the sense of never hurting anyone or their feelings, any more than it can be confused with politeness, though if we think of the basic meaning of the word *kindness,* they are indeed practically synonymous. The word is derived from the same root as *kin* and implies the standard of behavior required between primitive people of the same kin. This idea lived again in the debased external gentleman's code, which enforced courteous behavior to a man's own class and to no one else. The courtesy of the soul is lived only when every man as an individual person has been recognized as *kin*—and indeed when every animal and thing too is given the rights of kin in the oneness of creation. The courteous man is sensitively aware of the nature and need of the animal; recognizes with love and respect the infinitely varying functions of the different levels of life, animal, plant, and inanimate thing, and treats all with courtesy even when the demands of real values make unkindness in the ordinary sense a necessity.

Courtesy most emphatically does *not* mean covering up one's feelings in order to be superficially "kind." It does mean that these feelings are to be spoken out forthrightly and courageously in the appropriate place and to the appropriate people. If, however, the personal negative feelings that seize us all from time to time are allowed to swamp us in a mood, and to permeate the atmosphere, then obviously we must lose all respect and concern for the individuals around us and, even if we do not speak a word, we are guilty of discourtesy. We are then enclosed in a private world, and for the moment people don't exist except in the mass or as a projection point for our bad feeling. Thus we evade the pain of fact, in a family or in any household or group. The existence of such a mood, uncontained, in one individual, or an unresolved conflict between two members of a household can invade the atmosphere and disturb the free flow of courtesy and attention between each and all. One does not need to be talking to someone in order to maintain the offer of full attention.

These thoughts bring to light another paradox at the heart of courtesy. It is born of the union of austere discipline and complete spontaneity. A spontaneous, joyful feeling is engendered by the mere presence of a courteous person, but someone who is simply impulsive, at the mercy of thoughtless, undisciplined moods, can never bring forth the free spontaneity of real courtesy.

Another kind of courtesy that is valid is the respect due to a person's function or rank. This can of course become hypocritical and distasteful if it is not joined to the deeper person-to-person courtesy of which we have spoken. Where there is discrimination of the individual value, there will be the true respect for the function, no matter how much the person carrying it may be disliked. Courtesy is good taste in human behavior.

We will conclude with four examples of various kinds of courtesy. To the readers of Rex Stout's Nero Wolfe stories, their peculiar fascination lies in the fact that whereas he has no soft and charming manners and never indulges in "kind" circumlocutions, he is invariably and profoundly a man of courtesy. In him it shows mainly under the aspect of the second of the knightly virtues we have discussed—a complete honesty and integrity and consistency. He tells endless lies as a necessity of his job, in his search for the ultimate truth of each situation, but he is never untrue to his vision of the dignity of man. He makes no pretense of chivalry and doing good. He is out to make money and work at his job when he must. Yet the moment he feels that courtesy has laid an obligation on him, he will put out exactly the same effort with not a penny of reward—even to going without his beloved food! There is one story in which a dog has put himself under Archie's protection, and courtesy to the dog commands Nero's utmost efforts. He also shows an extreme sense of courtesy to the English language—a very rare kind of good manners nowadays!

In Tolstoy's *War and Peace* there are some beautiful passages describing what is essentially the transformation of a truly good, kind man, into a courteous man. Pierre in his early life was invariably kind and polite, full of plans to free his serfs, intent on his search for the meaning of life, but nevertheless he makes everyone he meets uneasy and his good schemes always go awry through his lack of discrimination. He goes through a time of great suffering as a prisoner of the French, and meets, in conditions of terrible hardship, an ignorant peasant who is nevertheless a completely whole man, simple and selfless, living each moment in its fullness. Pierre emerges from this experience transformed. Now whomever he meets—whether an embittered spinster, an avid intellectual, his servants, or his pompous doctor—each one of them begins to reveal his best side, instead of his worst. Each one, not knowing why, loves to be with Pierre, who talks very little himself (whereas before he was forever making speeches about his ideals) but draws out the other with understanding and genuine interest. Of the new attitude Tolstoy writes:

> This was his acknowledgment of the impossibility of changing a man's convictions by words, and his recognition of the possibility of everyone thinking, feeling, and seeing things each from his own point of view. This legitimate peculiarity of each individual, which used to excite and irritate Pierre, now became a basis of the sympathy he felt for, and the interest he took in, other people.[2]

This kind of mature courtesy can surely only be reached through deep suffering.

Those who knew the late Charles Williams spoke always of the beauty and power of his courtesy. Here is a quotation from C.S. Lewis:

> The highest compliment I ever heard paid to them (Williams' manners) was by a nun. She said that Mr. Williams' manners implied a complete *offer* of intimacy without the slightest *imposition* of intimacy. He threw down all his barriers without ever implying that you should lower yours. . . . He gave to every circle the whole man: all his attention, knowledge, courtesy, charity, were placed at your disposal. . . . This total offer of himself but without that tacit claim which so often accompanies such offers, made his friendship the least exacting in the world, and explains the surprising width of his contacts. One kept on discovering that the most unlikely people loved him as well as we did.[3]

Finally, a paragraph from John Moore's novel *The Waters Under the Earth*—a father is thinking about his daughter:

> Ferdo had noticed that she got on particularly well with proud, independent, awkward characters such as Egbert and Fenton, and he thought it was because she had courtesy, which implied a great deal more than civility and good manners. It meant that while being completely *your*self, you were all the time helping the other person to be *him*self, through your appreciation of his point of view, your respect for his individuality, your sensibility and and your quick awareness of how he thought and felt and

and and your quick awareness of how he thought and felt and what he was. You could show courtesy to animals too. When Susan picked up a hedgehog off the road, to save it from being run over, when she handled a kitten or a toad or an injured bird or a grass-snake, she seemed to know how it liked to be held, to be aware of its special fears and discomforts, in fact to appreciate all the things which made that particular creature different from other creatures. It sometimes seemed to Ferdo that courtesy was an uncommon thing nowadays, and welcome as a spring flower.[4]

6

The King and the Principles of the Heart

I f we interpret the image of the king in a dream and fairy tale as the leading principle of collective consciousness, and leave it at that, we surely risk draining that rich image of its manna and reducing it to a mere concept. It is, of course, true that the death of the old king and the immediate succession of the new, whether in myth or in the dream of an individual, means that a new ruling attitude to life is dawning; whereas the sick or wounded king, as in the Grail legend, shows that the change is overdue—the old leading principle is dying but cannot finally disappear because the new "king" has not yet been found, and is not yet ready, is still too weak, too unconscious, to take up his rule.

What is it, however, that distinguishes the king from all other kinds of rulers or leaders? What is the "royal" thing in each man's unconscious? It is not only a matter of the carrying of immense responsibility for the lives of others—all true rulers must do that. That which is essential to a king and to no other leader is his *inherited* right to kingship. All aristocracies, also, were founded on inherited rights, but aristocracy is an offshoot of royalty and loses its meaning as an institution as soon as the monarchy is destroyed. Why, then, does the power conferred by inheritance carry a manna that never attaches to any other kind of leader, however great and powerful? The power of a Hitler, or of a Napoleon even (who merely called himself a king), to inspire fanatical devotion has a different origin. It depends on the personality of the leader, whereas the devotion inspired by a king, though it may be greatly intensified or weakened by the personality of the monarch, is not fundamentally dependent on the king as a man. It derives from the spontaneous reverence in all human beings who are not cut off from their instinctive roots for the archetype of kingship, for the royalty that is passed on from father to son for generations. The manna lies precisely in the fact that a king is not a king because of personal merit or demerit but because he is of the "blood royal," that is, he carries symbolically in his body the essence of the experience, responsibility, and nobility of the ancestors. The word *aristocracy* means "the rule of the best," and a king will be true to his kingship insofar as he is faithful to the "best," never substituting the second best, never identifying his ego with his royalty. If he interprets his great inheritance from the ancestors in the light of the "best" of his own age, he then becomes the symbol, not only of the stored riches of the past, but of the new consciousness of the present and of that which gives birth to the hidden seed of the future, the heir to the throne.

Jung said that the unconscious of man is aristocratic, and it follows that the image of the true ruler therein is the king. It is interesting that of all modern leaders, the Kennedys came nearest in America to inspiring the numinous feeling belonging to kingship—and it was surely because of the quality of inherited aristocracy that people felt in them—so that the phrase "the Kennedy dynasty" was often heard. Whether spoken with contempt or approval, it betrays the concern of the unconscious with kingship.

The king as ruler in the modern world has practically disappeared. He no longer belongs in our collective culture. He survives only in one or two countries where he does not rule but still carries the symbol of royalty. In England the monarchy is still, for many, a living symbol because of the genius of the English for slow, nonviolent change, and because of the extraordinary vitality in their unconscious of the aristocratic tradition embodied in the Arthurian myth—a myth that has been filled with new vitality by succeeding generations of poets. The monarchy therefore remains a living symbol of the unity behind the multiplicity of party politics. But the king, in his full power and majesty, no longer walks on the conscious stage of our world. "The king," we may say, "is dead," and yet though we do not speak it aloud, are not aware of it even, a voice in our hearts completes the ritual sentence. "The king is dead; long live the king!"

For the king cannot die, and having disappeared from outer life, his image in the unconscious takes on a greatly increased power and it becomes the task of each man and woman to find his or her own individual relationship to the royal image within. The disappearance of a valid outer collective projection point for an archetype will mean for the many a repression of its power and meaning, and result in negative and meaningless projections of that power; but for some it is a great opportunity, a call to the transformation of the hitherto projected image into an attribute of individual consciousness.

The "blood royal," then, in each of us is that which inherits the high responsibility of *ruling* in the psyche, of uniting the personality in the service of the "best." It is that which is born anew in every individual and carries the deposit of all the experience of selfless leadership that the kings among men have garnered through the long ages of the struggle toward consciousness. We cannot evade or refuse this inheritance of the blood. It is not won or earned; it is born in us, yet it must be discovered and taken up consciously by each new heir, who must submit to long training and self-discipline if he is not to betray his calling and become either a tyrant, using his power to hurt or destroy, or a weak king at the mercy of the petty power-seekers around him—that is, of all the little hidden greeds and plots of the ego.

The story of Aragorn in *The Lord of the Rings* is a beautiful study of the royal power in man. For generations his forbears had been in exile, so that the kingdom of Gondor, though ably ruled by stewards, was sinking slowly into decay, lacking that irreplaceable thing, the manna of the king. When the kingly function is repressed, the leadership of the psyche either falls into the hands of self-seeking factions at war with each other, or a man may be ruled for a long time by the second best—by motives, ideas, feelings, fine and good in themselves and administered by a noble "steward." Nothing, however, can arrest a gradual decay such as took place in Gondor except the return of the king, that indefinable power whose sanction lies beyond all rational thought and good government. It may even be said that a king who betrays his high calling is a more positive thing in the psyche than the excellent rulers who are not kings, for, however corrupted, he carries the seed of royalty and sooner or later he will give birth to the heir who will restore the true meaning of kingship. But if there is no king, then the "white tree" in the psyche dies and the seed lies dormant for the duration of the exile.

"How many hundreds of years needs it to make a steward a king, if the king returns not?" asks Boromir of his father, the steward. And Denethor replied, "Few years, may be, in other places of less royalty. In Gondor ten thousand years would not suffice."[1] For there are greater and lesser kingdoms, greater and lesser kings. Aristocratic stewardship may take on the quality of royalty in lesser matters, but the great kingdoms of the soul must wait for the heir to the ancient line of kings, reaching back and down to the origins of life.

The King of Kings in the Christian creed is Christ. He rules in the Kingdom of Heaven within, which is the totality, and his words to Pilate speak with peculiar force to the individual in this age, when the image of kingship is debased or ignored. "If my kingdom were of this world, then would my servants fight." When the king is known in his true nature *within,* there is an end to conflict, an end to war in the psyche. "Thou sayest that I am a King. To this end was I born and for this came I into the world that I should bear witness unto the truth; everyone that is of the truth heareth my voice" (John 18:36f.).

It is the simplest and most profound definition of kingship. At the moment of his condemnation to death as a common criminal, Christ proclaims the king within who brings unity by his devotion to *truth.* The essential for each man and woman, then, groping along his or her way, is to find the "king" in the psyche who embodies *his own truth* at any given moment of his life, and to give complete allegiance to him, accepting also the certainty that this king must die at his appointed time to give place to his heir, for until we come consciously into the kingdom of the King of Kings, of the Self, there will be a long succession of lesser kings of varying degrees of fallibility but passing on nevertheless the seed of truth until we can say, each person of him or herself, "to this end was I born." To quote again the words of Charles Williams, "Unless devotion is given to that which proves false in the end, that which is true in the end cannot enter.'' This is why the *passionate* sinner has always been seen by the wise as nearer to the kingdom of heaven than the respectable do-gooder; there is a king somewhere in him, however corrupted, not a politician, in control, for he is wholly given over to his passion, and he does not plot and calculate his gains and losses.

It is, then vitally important that we seek constantly to be aware of what kind of ruler is governing our lives. Are we giving allegiance to a mere demagogue or politician, elected to serve the conscious needs of the moment or the purposes of the ego? Or is our ruler, perhaps, a steward or statesman, devoted to the good as he sees it, in which case our danger is that we see no need for the king or forget that he exists? Or is he a true king, whose authority derives from royalty of blood and royalty of spirit and whose reign brings a basic unity to the personality? No matter, then, if we must wait long for his return from exile for his effectiveness to be felt in our lives, provided we do not forget him nor supercede him, but act as stewards of his high responsibility as best we may.

When the king is the true heir, then always in all the kingdoms of the world those who give allegiance must do so unto death. There can be no conditional allegiance. As without, so within, for the king is an objective leading principle, the ruler who carries the authority of our own truth, and when it is time for a new king to succeed to the old, a conscious dying of the old is required, as was foreshadowed in the ritual killing of the king in antiquity and in all the myths of the death and dismemberment of the king. If we have given this full devotion to our king, then when his time is over the heir will be ready, but if we have been split and divided, as all the people of goodwill had become divided in the Ring story, the king may remain sick or wounded or in exile for a long time, while we await the birth of an heir and his slow growing to maturity. At Parsifal's first coming to the grail castle and meeting with the wounded king, in his green youth, he had no notion of the meaning of it all, but immediately after this glimpse he knew for the first time his own name and the nature of his quest and accepted the long road he must travel to achieve it. So also did Aragorn.

Aragorn's father died when he was a boy, so that he became a king before he even knew of his inheritance, for he was not told of it until he was a young man. His mother took him to Rivendell where he passed his boyhood with Elrond and his sons, absorbing the truths both of this world and of the eternal life of the Imagination embodied by the Elves, for in Elrond ran the blood of both elf and man. So he received the essential education of a true king, whereby he learned to accept the validity of both conscious and unconscious, of both spirit and blood.

Here in Rivendell at his coming of age he became aware of himself, of his high destiny for good or ill, and was given the broken sword. Always in myth the potential king finds or is given his sword at the moment of his passing from unconscious boyhood to conscious manhood—he awakens to the realization of his fate, of his inheritance. The sword may be found, or, if broken, reforged, only by its rightful owner. Arthur alone could draw Excalibur from the stone, Siegfried alone could reforge Nothung, and Aragorn alone must carry the broken Anduril until the time of its reforging.

What does it mean that the sword of the king within us may be broken when first it comes into his hand? There may come a moment in the life of a man, often when he is quite young, in which he glimpses with a strange feeling of certainty that which will be the dominant task, the leading principle of his whole life. It may present itself as a specific career, or as an urge to achieve a certain kind of insight, or knowledge or creative work; in a word, he has glimpsed his unique task in this world. For some this results in an immediate wielding of the sword, a setting to work at once on the way which is theirs. But there are others whose fate it is to take up the *broken* sword. Such a man may find himself mistaken as to the actual way in which he imagines himself living out this first insight of the meaning of his life. The vision may perhaps grow dim among the pressures of necessity and triviality, or even be totally lost; but if he has in truth taken up at that moment the sword, broken though it is—if at the root of his being the will has accepted the long years of preparation, of drudgery perhaps, of failures and false starts, consenting to carry the broken sword of the king in exile rather than wield a bright blade that may bring immediate success and recognition, then the king, the highest and noblest ruling principle of his life, may in his due time become the ruler of a great kingdom whose boundaries reach beyond earth and sky.

The first thing that happens to Aragorn after his awakening is that he meets Arwen, daughter of Elrond and granddaughter of

Galadriel, the great Elven queen, in the woods at Rivendell, and knows that he loves her and will do so to the end. And so we are at the outset reminded that there is no true king without a queen. Without her the line is sterile—the leading principle is cut off from the earth, from the heart, from human relationship. His power may be great, he may conquer great realms of the mind, but he is doomed to ultimate destruction, for no heir can be born to him.

For Aragorn, for the king of the broken sword, there can be no immediate union with his lady. She still belongs to the Elven world, she is not mortal; she is a vision and a hope, and only after he has endured loneliness and discipline and years of obscure work does she make the vital choice to become human, to accept mortality, and so becomes a woman and his promised queen. He is only now ready for the great fight with the Dark Lord and the winning of his kingdom. In those who may come at the last to high maturity, the great king who will finally take up his rule in them may remain for a long time in obscurity because the queen who will render him fertile and connect him to the earth is still an ideal, alive only in the Elven world of the imagination. There is great danger for such a man, who has vividly experienced the anima in her elf nature, that she will remain always remote from the earth, that she will, as it were, choose immortality, in which case his life on earth will remain crippled and sterile, his greatest potentiality unrealized. It is equally fatal, of course, if, in choosing mortality, she forgets or denies her elf blood. Arwen did neither. The *hierosgamos,* the marriage of king and queen, which is the symbol of the final unity of Heaven and Earth, can never be experienced if the queen remains a numinous image, refusing full incarnation.

The king in a woman's psyche is not substantially different from his image in a man's. He is for her, as for him, the leading principle of her being to which she gives allegiance, but he manifests himself in different ways. Obviously, a woman who is possessed by a multiplicity of animi has not found the king at all. She spends her life in the atmosphere of a party convention, proclaiming the inalienable truth of one set of opinions and denouncing all who oppose them; or else she is at the mercy of her emotions, bending to every wind that blows, unable to utter a clear "yes" or "no." But if she has found an objective truth that is *her* truth for any given time of her life and has the courage to live by it, she has found the king, and he will show himself in her life rather in a great enrichment of her femininity than in a wielding of the sword in her outer life. For the animus, whether king or commoner, is for a woman that which relates her to her unconscious mind; and the king in her psyche must indeed take up, or reforge, his sword, but he wields it in the service of her creativity in the *inner* world; and so her function of true feminine relatedness is freed from the plots by which it is distorted when her inferior masculinity rules from below without a true king to lead and command. Then, if this is her way, she can enter the masculine world with a creative strength of spirit peculiarly her own.

We may here note that it is not by chance that in our time the symbol of the royal leading principle is carried by a queen in both England and Holland. In this century the overwhelming need of mankind is to rediscover the *royal* nature of the feminine values. This is not the place for a discussion of the queen image in matriarchal times and the necessary centuries of patriarchal supremacy. In our time the queen is emerging into possible conscious union with the king image.

Aragorn's years of training are spent in incessant work for the protection of people to whom his care is unknown. It is a slow training in the selfless responsibility that is the essential quality of a king; and so it is with every man and woman in whom the royal nature comes finally to light. He grows into the realization that in everything he is, and in everything he does, he carries responsibility for all men. Royalty of nature is a clearly recognizable thing. It shows itself in a kind of dignity, an unafraid acceptance of responsibility in great things and in small; an assured authority that never seeks to dominate, but is rather an attribute of character. "He speaks as one having authority and not as the Scribes" (Matt. 7:29). The scribes were "the authorities," but the carpenter's son was a king.

H.C. Goddard points out how Shakespeare from his early plays onward was concerned with this matter of true royalty, seeing it, as did very few in his age, as an inner quality, not as something necessarily attached to outer kingship. In *King John* it is the bastard Faulconbridge, who is the kingly man, the actual king being no better than a childish weakling. Goddard writes:

"Look at them," Shakespeare seems to say as he places them side by side. "A man is greater than a king." But there is another kind of king, and in that sense Faulconbridge is king of "king John." That is the irony of the title. . . . The king is a bastard. He hasn't even the ordinary title of son. *His title is the truth.* If ever a play brought the mere name of king, the institution of royalty, into disrepute, it is this one. But in behalf of no shallow egalitarianism— for after all, Faulconbridge has royal blood in his veins.[2]

Thus Shakespeare preserves the symbolism of the blood royal, while exposing the emptiness of the mere institution.

In its early stages, however, the kingly quality in a man is easily misunderstood by those who do not look below the surface. "Strider" was Aragorn's name to most people, and they were suspicious of his apparently aimless comings and goings, and of his aloofness. They had no idea what they owed to him. And "Strider" he chose to remain even when he came into his kingdom, taking it as his simple family name to balance his great titles. So also it is the mark of the person in whom the kingly nature lives that he remains at the same time entirely simple and without pretension. It is significant that Aragorn's first moment of choice after he took on the leadership of the company was between the following of the direct road to his kingdom and the turning aside to rescue the two insignificant hobbits from their captors. He chose the latter and so proved himself a true king, who had found his queen, the values of his heart.

There is another quality whereby one may recognize the king. Ioreth, the old woman of Gondor, said, "The hands of a king are the hands of a healer." This is an ancient belief, founded on yet another of those deep paradoxes of the unconscious that shock us into awareness. He who wields the sword and sceptre of truth carries healing in his hands. His responsibility is not only to lead, to direct, to uphold justice and mercy, but to make men whole from those diseases of the soul which all the science of the doctor cannot reach. In medieval England the disease that the touch of the king could heal when all else failed was scrofula—and it was called, interestingly, "the king's evil," a hint that the origin of the disease lies in the shadow side of royalty. Scrofula is a degenerative, wasting disease.

In *The Lord of the Rings* the sickness that none but the king may heal comes from the wounds inflicted by that other and dark king, the Lord of the Ringwraiths. This king is precisely a wraith, a great ruler who has betrayed his kingship, delivering it over to the purposes of Sauron and the dark destructive power, and in so doing all his humanity has wasted away—he no longer has form or face as a man. The wounds he inflicts have therefore the power to infuse a deadly cold into the body and to pull a man gradually away from life and warmth, so that his will is poisoned and he falls into unconsciousness and death. No science of medicine and healing can ever reach these wounds. Even the sage is powerless to heal them. Gandalf can do nothing for those who lie dying from the wounds of the ghost king, for their *will* is failing, and they hear no human voice now except the voice of *command* of the true king, halting them as they waste away, arousing them to response, restoring their will to live, which derives from the authority of the king within. "I have called him back," says Aragorn.

So when a man feels himself in the grip of this disease of the will, it is of no use to analyze the symptoms or apply ordinary psychological techniques. Let him rather call on the king through his imagination, summon the buried royal man in himself, with his power to command response to reality and to awareness of responsibilities, however seemingly trivial. If he does not do this, his danger is extreme, for he gradually fades, no matter how great his insights and his knowledge, until he walks the world like an empty shell.

The relationship between Aragorn and Gandalf is an image of the altogether different functions of the king and the sage. They may be easily confused, for Gandalf is the supreme leader in the war of the Ring, and Aragorn defers to him in all the greatest decisions. Yet, though he leads and points the way, it is the king who commands and Gandalf himself could have done little without the authority of the king—not only Aragorn's but Theoden's authority too.

Gandalf's awakening of Theoden from his blind subservience to Wormtongue makes this very clear. Only Theoden could arouse his people and lead them to the fight, just as only Gandalf could break the spell that was destroying Theoden's kingly nature. The sage is the deepest wisdom within us, the vision of the eternal truths of the spirit, but the king alone can turn our vision into decisive action here and now.

In the story of Theoden lies a warning of how the kingly function may be subtly undermined. There is a "Wormtongue" in all of us, whispering doubt as to our strength, counseling prudence and compromise in all the wrong places, telling us we are too weak to make clear decisions that may prove mistaken or to take up this or that responsibility, that we cannot draw the sword and stand firm—for all sorts of speciously sensible reasons. Then there is hope only in the coming of a Gandalf who will strike the scales from our eyes. But no wisdom, no vision will serve unless there is a king to govern and to command in the service of that wisdom.

The two images of sage and king recur often in the *I Ching* and they make clear the distinction. Here are some examples[3]:

In the sign of The Ting, the Cauldron, the sixth and top line is the sage, but the fifth line is the *ruler* of the hexagram. The commentary points out that it is only possible for the sage to impart his teachings because the ruler meets him halfway with receptivity.

Again in the hexagram of The Well, the top line, the sage, symbolizes the rising of the water to the top of the well, making it possible for all to draw it, but the fifth line is the ruler, and the commentary states that water in a well is useless if it is not drawn out, and it is the active task of the ruler to take action so that others may drink. The third line reads: "The well is cleaned but no one drinks from it. This is my heart's sorrow. For one might drink from it. If the King were clear-minded, good fortune might be enjoyed in common."

The hexagram of Dispersion, Dissolution deals with times of breaking up and of reuniting on a new level. For this the essential is clearly a king. The judgment reads: "Dispersion—Success—the King approaches his temple." It is not enough for the temple to be there, the king must lead the people or the psyche into it. The fifth line tells us that the king is in his proper place, the ruling place, and that therefore he can inspire the people with a great idea that will be the focal point of unity after dissolution.

The *I Ching* also sees the king in the simple daily matters of relationship. The ruling line in the sign of The Family reads: "As a King he approaches his family. Fear not. . . . They associate with one another in love." If the authority in a family has a quality of *royalty* it will be maintained, not by severity and through fear, but through the love and willing devotion with which a true king is always surrounded.

The king comes into "his proper place" (to use the *I Ching* phrase) at his crowning, and the crown symbolizes, as do all rings, a total commitment. When, at the end Aragorn is crowned, the crown is set on his head by Gandalf, but it is carried to Gandalf by Frodo, the simple, down-to-earth hobbit who has borne the greatest burden of all, who has carried that other ring of power without binding himself to it, without using it, a thing that neither king nor sage could have done. So always, in fact, has a king been crowned. The holy man, the sage, who is the greatest in the realm of the spirit, places on the king's head the symbol of the whole, of the new king's total commitment to the highest *truth,* or vision of the Self, possible in his time. "To this end was I born." The crown, however, is, in the last analysis, brought to him by the common people on whose devotion his kingdom depends. In other words, the authority and majesty of the king within us rests finally on the consent and love that we give to him in the simplest, most ordinary, everyday acts. So we bring the crown to the king, to that within us that inherits the truth of the past, interprets the truth of the present, and gives birth to the truth of the future.

Isaiah describes a man whose feet are planted on a rock and whose daily nourishment of simple bread and water never fails, and he says of him, "Thine eyes shall see the King in his beauty; they shall behold the land that is very far off" (Isa. 33:17).

7

It's of No Consequence: The Joy of the Fool

I remember that, during a discussion of Charles Williams's novel *The Greater Trumps* some time ago, someone asked for a definition of "The Fool." It was, of course, not forthcoming, for The Fool of the Tarot eludes all analysis. If he could be rationally defined, he would cease to be The Fool. This is true, in fact, of any numinous symbol. When we perceive an image in the immediacy of imaginative vision, it glows with a undying vitality and changes our lives, but as soon as we insist on a rational understanding of it, the symbol is dead.

The always dreary occultist definitions of the symbolism of the Greater Trumps are worse than boring in the case of The Fool; they deprive him of all his meaning. Only the poet, inarticulate in most of us, can reveal to us The Fool, and our perception is sharpened, our vision intensified by response to those great men of poetic genius who have now and then created specific human images in whom The Fool is incarnate. I would like to say something about four of these fools and so try to evoke a little of their magic. Each is as completely different from all the others as can be, yet, in all, the essential reality of The Fool is vividly alive. The four poets are Shakespeare, Wordsworth, Dickens, and Charles Williams. The four characters are King Lear, The Idiot

Boy, Mr. Toots in *Dombey and Son,* and Sybil in *The Greater Trumps.*

Charles Williams alone has written about the actual image of The Fool of the Tarot, and nothing can awaken us more surely to the difference between head knowledge and vision than to go straight from a perusal of the usual "explanations" of the cards to a reading of the scene in *The Greater Trumps* where Sybil is first shown the tiny golden images of the Tarot moving unceasingly on the round table.

The image of The Fool, in the version of the cards used by nineteenth-century and modern occultists, is a picture of a young man stepping gaily and fearlessly, without looking where he is going, to the edge of a precipice. Over his right shoulder he holds a wand with a bag on the end of it; in his left hand is a white rose and at his feet a little dog stands on his hind legs. The signs of the Zodiac are on his belt and other symbolic designs are on his tunic. In the French Marseille version the figure is much simpler and there are many fewer symbols. We see The Fool from behind and he looks back over his right shoulder; the dog, if it is a dog, is tearing a rent in his trouser leg. There is evidence that the animal was originally a white lynx (Williams calls it a tiger) biting The Fool's left calf; so we may think of it as an animal both wild and domestic. The card is unnumbered, marked 0. It has been variously placed, by those who failed to understand, at the beginning, at the end, or between cards 20 and 21, but it is plain that it does not belong in the series at all—that it is quite separate from the numbered trumps and yet, we may add, essential to each. It is nowhere and everywhere.

A sample of the usual kind of interpretation is found in a little book published by the School of Ageless Wisdom, of Los Angeles. "The wreath around The Fool's head symbolizes the vegetable kingdom; also Victory. The wand is Will, the Wallet memory. The white rose represents purified desire. . . ." and so on.[1]

The Fool has also been described as the Cosmic Life Breath about to descend into the Abyss of Manifestation. There is nothing inaccurate in these pompous statements; there is simply no imaginative truth in them. They "darken counsel by words without knowledge" and The Fool remains motionless, a dead picture in our minds. So in Charles Williams' story the little golden figure of The Fool with the tiger leaping beside him remained, for all but one of the watchers, unmoving in the center of the table, while the other images moved in a kind of patternless dance around him. Mr. Coningsby (the narrow-minded, self-centered extravert) says,

> "Why doesn't the one in the middle dance?"
> "We imagine that its weight and position must make it a kind of counterpoise," Henry answered.
> "Has he a tiger by him for any particular reason?" Mr. Coningsby inquired. "Fools and tigers seem a funny conjunction."
> "Nobody knows about the Fool," Aaron burst in.
> Then Sybil spoke: "I can't see this central figure," she said. "Where is it exactly . . . ?"
> Then Henry turned to her with great eagerness. "Miss Coningsby, can you see the Fool and his tiger at all?"
> She surveyed the table carefully. "Yes," she said at last, "There—no, there—no—it's moving so quickly I can hardly see it—there—ah, it's gone again. Surely that's it, dancing with the rest; it seems as if it were always arranging itself in some place which was empty for it . . . it certainly seems to be dancing everywhere."[2]

He is dancing everywhere, always dancing in the place which is empty for him, and the tiger, the dog, dances with him; and where they dance there is order and peace of a kind that the world calls folly or idiocy or sheer madness; but only those who, like Sybil, have come to live from that center of order and peace can see him dance at all times and in all places—the dance which is the joy of the universe. "Never forget," says R.H. Blyth, "all joy is idiot joy—all love is idiot love."[3] And he quotes from Shakespeare: "The lunatic, the lover, and the poet are of imagination all compact."[4] The lover or the poet who knows not lunacy—the dance of The Fool—is never in truth a lover or a poet at all.

Sybil Coningsby in Williams' novel is a woman who, through years of interior suffering, living a most ordinary outer life without any dramatic experiences visible to the world, has come in full consciousness to the state of "complete simplicity, costing not less than everything," as T.S. Eliot describes it.[5] She does nothing *for* anyone anymore; she does not teach or plan; yet her every word or action spontaneously and inevitably transforms each situation in which she is involved from chaotic movement into an ordered dance—a dance of "idiotic" joy, even when, as in the great magical storm of the book, the destruction of the world is threatened. For she moves in unison with, in Williams' words, "that which has no number and is called The Fool, because man finds it folly till it is known. It is sovereign or it is nothing, and if it is nothing, then man was born dead."[6]

Sybil is the only one of the four characters mentioned above who is portrayed as being in *conscious* relationship to The Fool. Yet in spite of the beauty and depth of Williams' writing, she falls, perhaps, short of the others in the power to awaken response to The Fool in our unconscious. There is something contrived about her, as though Williams were concerned to create *a* woman in this state of wholeness instead of *the* living human being called Sybil Coningsby. This would, in most fiction, be a fatal weakness, but Charles Williams' novels are dramas of the inner world—myths rather than novels proper—and his own experience of that world is so intense that it reaches us through his characters in spite of their lack of human characterization.

Nevertheless, Shakespeare, Wordsworth, and Dickens do a greater thing for those with ears to hear. They create absolutely real, unique human beings whose unconscious folly is so divine that, as we read with the understanding of the heart, The Fool is roused from his immobility and dances within us, and for a moment his secret is ours, not spoken, not known, but experienced.

The actual "fools" of Shakespeare's plays do not carry the image of The Fool. The ancient institution of the court jester was surely born of the instinctive knowledge that the wisdom of this world must always maintain contact with the true fool if it is not to swallow those who wield power. The court fool, however, was more often simply a privileged wit speaking home truths to the ruler, balancing the solemnity surrounding a king. In Shakespeare, sometimes he is a heartless spinner of words, like Touchstone; sometimes a truly wise, tender, and fearless heart like the fool in *King Lear*. Lear's fool is wise and kind, seeing clearly the stupidity of the king before the madness comes upon him, but it is Lear himself turned mad who at the end of the play embodies *The* Fool, the divine insanity of the "simple" recognized by the ancients as holy, but by us despised and lumped together with all the other kinds of madness.

The storm of suffering that breaks the reason of the king, sweeping away all the calculating, blind stupidity of his ego-sanity, leaves him at the end a fool indeed. "He knows not what he says," remarks Albany—but all his words are Truth, not reason. His speech about life in prison, his final "delusion" in the eyes of the world that Cordelia lives are, as Goddard so movingly writes in his wonderful chapter on *King Lear,* truths of the imagination—not transitory facts.[7] When at the end Lear accepts for a moment the "fact" that Cordelia is truly dead, he exclaims, "and my poor fool is hang'd." Goddard suggests that the fool of the play and Cordelia are "wedded" in his mind, since we cannot imagine him calling his daughter "fool" at this point. It could be even deeper than this; it could be that for him to have accepted the rational fact of Cordelia's death at this supreme moment—to have denied the imaginative truth of his folly whereby he knew she was immortal—would have been indeed the death of *The* Fool, and when *The* Fool dies for a man, nothing is left but meaningless despair. If we imagine the play without the intense cry of joy at the end, *"Look on her, look, her lips, look there, look there,"* we realize the greatness of Shakespeare's genius. Lear dies a Fool and because of this all the terror—the appalling pain—of the play is infused with hope instead of despair.

It is for us to choose. Either we know with King Lear the truth that Cordelia in her absolute integrity and innocence is immortal, or we see only the final delusion of a tragic and broken old man. This truth is, moreover, not a statement that the abstract qualities that Cordelia typified survive all disasters; it is a vision of the same order as Dante sang of with such passionate joy when he met Beatrice in Heaven. She is a symbol, yes, but she is also the same human girl whom he met in the streets of Florence. "Look well, we are, we are Beatrice." King Lear wins through in his last moment to "idiot love" and "idiot joy."

With that other great fool, Don Quixote, it is otherwise. We do not know why Cervantes should appear at the end to have lost faith in his vision when he shows his hero dying sane and repenting his follies. Either he did not understand his own creation or else he consciously wrote this scene to make unmistakably clear the paucity of factual reality in the face of the glory of imaginative truth. It is a shocking thing to read the last chapter. Even the hitherto disapproving friends of Don Quixote implore him, as it were, not to betray his madness—and they are right. The splendor of the real Don

Quixote, however, survives this betrayal and few people remember the pitiful sane old man at the end. He is a pointless fact—not the truth of the man who attacked windmills.

From the folly of the old King Lear, his reason broken by suffering, his mind released into the wisdom of simplicity, we pass to "The Idiot Boy"—the child whose rational development is arrested, whose innocence remains untarnished by logic. Wordsworth's poem tells how the boy's mother, Betty, was terribly anxious one evening about her neighbor, an old woman named Susan Gale, who was very ill. She explained carefully to her idiot son, Johnny, that he must fetch the doctor from the village, setting him on their wise and gentle pony.

> And Betty's most essential charge
> Was "Johnny, Johnny, mind that you
> Come home again, not stop at all
> Come home again what ere befall,
>
> My Johnny do, I pray you, do."
> To this did Johnny answer make
> Both with his head and with his hand
> And proudly shook the bridle too.
> And then! His words were not a few
> Which Betty well could understand . . . .
>
> But when the Pony moved his legs
> Oh! then for the poor Idiot Boy!
> For joy he cannot hold the bridle
> For joy his head and heels are idle.
> He's idle all for very joy . . . .
>
> His heart it was so full of glee
> That, till fully fifty yards were gone,
> He quite forgot his holly whip
> And all his skill in horsemanship
> Oh! happy, happy, happy, John.

The evening wears on and Johnny does not return. His mother's anxiety grows and grows and rises to fever pitch when the clock strikes one. She must go out and find him and yet she hates to leave Susan, who is in great pain.

"I must be gone, I must away
Consider, Johnny's but half wise.
Susan, we must take care of him,
If he is hurt in life or limb."
"Oh God forbid," poor Susan cries.

And she urges the frantic Betty to go. The mother runs to the town; the doctor has not seen him. She even forgets to send the doctor to Susan and continues up onto the downs, into the woods, where the darkest imaginings as to his fate possess her.

Oh Reader! now that I might tell
What Johnny and his horse are doing!
What they've been doing all this time.
Oh could I put it into rhyme
A most delightful tale pursuing.

Perhaps, and no unlikely thought!
He with his Pony now doth roam
The Cliffs and Peaks so high that are,
To lay his hands upon a star
And in his pocket bring it home . . . .

Perhaps with head and heels on fire
And like the very soul of evil
He's galloping away, away,
And so will gallop on for aye,
The bane of all that dread the devil.

At last toward dawn she finds him beside a waterfall. Her joy knows no bounds. She cries and laughs.

She kisses o'er and o'er again
Him who she loves, her Idiot Boy;
She's happy here, is happy there,
She is uneasy everywhere;
Her limbs are all alive with joy.

She pats the Pony where or when
She knows not, happy Betty Foy.

The little Pony glad may be
But he is milder far than she
You hardly can perceive his joy.

"Oh Johnny never mind the Doctor
You've done your best and that is all."

The three turn homewards—and then comes the miracle—for in
the presence of idiot joy and idiot love there are always miracles. Hobbling up the road toward them comes old Susan Gale.
She had lain tossing on her bed in the grip of terrible fears for the
boy and his mother.

And as her mind grew worse and worse,
Her body still grew better.

"Alas! What is become of them?
These fears can never be endured.
I'll to the wood." The word scarce said
Did Susan rise up from her bed
As if by magic cured.

These two old women loved the fool, the boy who was of no
use, could earn no money, learn nothing, speak no interesting
facts, could not even be relied on to take a simple message, who
knew only the absolute sorrow of every moment. They loved
him beyond all thought of their own lives, their own pain. The
idiot came *first:* therefore the miracle.

It is when The Fool within us comes first—transcending all the
categories of reason—that miracles happen in our own lives.
When we are making frantic efforts to get rid of some inner pain
or conflict, to find, as it were, "the doctor" who will bring us
relief, how often we forget all about The Fool and his joy, and so
there is no empty place for him to dance in, and therefore no
hope of real cure. Certainly we may feel better more quickly, but
only to plunge again later on into the same darkness.

On the way home Betty returns to reason and asks Johnny to
tell her truly what he has been doing all night, what he has seen
and hears. Here are the last two verses.

Now Johnny all night long had heard
The owls in tuneful concert strive;
No doubt too he the moon had seen;
For in the moonlight he had been
From eight o'clock till five.

And thus to Betty's question he
Made answer, like a traveller bold,
(His very words I give to you.)
"The cocks did crow to-whoo to-whoo,
And the sun did shine so cold."

Thus answered Johnny in his glory,
And that was all his travel's story.

Lewis Carroll also knew "Johnny's glory"—

The sun was shining on the sea
Shining with all his might
He did his very best to make
The billows smooth and bright
And this was odd because it was
The middle of the night.

But not odd to Johnny and his kin—only to us, Who call it nonsense.

Last, but not least, we come to Charles Dickens, who is perhaps the greatest of all those who have brought alive for us The Fool in unforgettable characters. They are exaggerated—yes, larger than life (with a small "l") and often called caricatures—but they are instinct with the Life (with a capital "L"), which is far more real and enduring than the factual. Among the glorious company of Dickens' fools, for me at least, the most moving of all is Mr. Toots in *Dombey and Son*.

Whenever I think about Mr. Toots, I am apt to react just as Susan Nipper (Florence Dombey's maid) did when Mr. Toots came to the house. "Immediately I see that innocent in the hall, I burst out laughing first and then I choked." He induces a constant chuckle plus a lump in the throat, and the two together are pure idiotic delight. G.K. Chesterton says of him, "Nowhere else did Dickens express with such astonishing insight and truth his main contention, which is that to be good and idiotic is not a poor fate, but, on the contrary, an experience of primeval innocence, which wonders at all things." And again, Mr. Toots "always gets all the outside things of life wrong and all the inside things right."[8]

Mr. Toots, when we first meet him, is the "head boy" in Dr. Blimber's school for the education of "young gentlemen." The unfortunate boys from the age of six or so upwards are subjected to a forcing process, Latin and Greek being stuffed into them morning, noon, and night, until their brains are addled and their faces pale and glum. At some point along the way, Toots' unconscious had magnificently rebelled. Everything about Mr. Toots, by the way, could be said to be magnificent, from his gorgeous clothes, bought at that expensive tailor's establishment of Burgess and Company, to his humble diffidence and the love of his heart. Dickens' achievement is that while we laugh and laugh, we are in the same moment moved in the deepest way to love and to humility.

Mr. Toots is an orphan with plenty of money. He has a guardian, in the background, referred to by Toots as a "Pirate and a Corsair," whose only function is to hand over the money in due time. Apart from this shadowy figure, Mr. Toots stands alone in the world; we really cannot imagine him with ordinary parents and relations! At Dr. Blimber's his position was unique. He had a desk to himself and was allowed to occupy himself as he pleased since his brain refused to learn, and he spent much time writing long letters to himself from "Important People" like the Duke of Wellington! I wish Dickens had given us a sample of one of them. Everyone is his friend, from the tiny six-year-old Paul Dombey, whom he treated as an equal with solemn courtesy, to Mr. Feeder, B.A., and Dr. Blimber himself. The most surprising people will respect a true fool. His absolute honesty and guileless expectation of goodness in other people shame all but the completely ego-centered into some kind of recognition of the innocent goodness in him. The French philosopher Amiel wrote, "Nothing is more characteristic of a man than the way he behaves towards fools."

The forcing process of Dr. Blimber's, it would be said by the rational, had rendered Toots weak-minded. David Copperfield's Aunt, Betsy Trotwood, however, would certainly have said of him as she did of Mr. Dick, "His sagacity is wonderful." What sagacity indeed there is in the phrase that runs through Mr. Toots' conversation in all moments of stress. "It's of no consequence!"

We may imagine this phrase rising up for the first time from his unconscious in revolt at the stupidity of his education and asserting once and for all, "It's of no consequence!"—whereupon Toots' brain simply stopped registering unimportant facts, his mind and heart and spirit soared into freedom, and he became the absolutely unique and holy fool that he was and is.

Many of Dickens' characters repeat a phrase over and over again like a kind of theme song, a phrase that expresses the essence of each one's personality. Mr. Toots' phrase is profoundly apt; he has that rare and absolute humility that never for a moment *demands* a return, a consequence, a result, in any of his words or actions. Deeper yet, when we hear with a chuckle Mr. Toots saying, "It's of no consequence," in his moments of social embarrassment—often in wildly inappropriate situations—somehow we are set free for a moment and glimpse that joyful state beyond cause and effect where nothing at all has any consequence. "It's of no consequence" has quite a different flavor from, "It doesn't matter" or "I don't care," for the word *consequence* means a result following an action. When we are briefly aware that *nothing* has any consequence, we are beyond time dancing with The Fool in an idiot joy.

The operation of this unconscious, timeless knowledge in Mr. Toots is manifested paradoxically, as it always is, in the marvelous timing of all his actions. He is always there at exactly the right moment without thought or plan. In those rare moments when we are free of the shackles of cause and effect, we move in tune with the synchronicity of the universe and make no mistakes. Mr. Toots just happens to be there, when only he could bring help. He is there to take care of Susan when that brave, soft-hearted, little spitfire is sent away from Florence after telling Mr. Dombey what she thinks of him; he is there to ease the shock when Walter, supposed drowned, returns; he is there to find Susan again in Florence's need. Best of all, he is there to comfort Florence after little Paul's death, bringing with him the rough and unprepossessing mongrel that Paul had loved at Blimber's as a present for the utterly lonely girl. Weak-minded he may be, unable to get names right, vague as can be on all matters of fact, but the delicacy of perception in that simple act is far beyond the kindness of reasonable minds. Diogenes, the boisterous dog, so unsuitable a pet for a lady in those days, literally saved Florence from despair. Mr. Toots always has his values straight. "I say, Miss Dombey, I could have had him stolen for ten shillings, if they hadn't given him up, and I would. . . !"

The fascinating thing is that on the conscious level Mr. Toots is always "kidding himself" as we should say, that he happens to be there—happens to be passing the house at just the moment when Florence is going out—and he expresses great surprise at the coincidence, when in reality he daily walks past in the hope of seeing her. This does not alter—it somehow enhances—the reality of the unconscious, happening to be there at crucial moments. Mr. Toots is in love—deeply, truly, and idiotically in love with Florence. He gets himself into all kinds of hilarious meshes of words and ridiculous situations on account of this love, and again we laugh with delight at his embarrassments and cry with delight over the delicacy, tenderness, and selflessness of his idiot love.

During this time, "richly dressed for the purpose," he would incessantly leave cards at Mr. Dombey's door. Then, as though it were an afterthought, he would ask for Susan. When she came, "How de do?" Mr. Toots would say with a chuckle and a blush. Susan would answer that she was very well. "How's Diogenes going on?" would be Mr. Toots' second interrogation. "Very well indeed. Miss Florence was fonder of him every day." Mr. Toots was sure to hail this with a burst of chuckles, "like the opening of a bottle of some effervescent beverage." "Miss Florence is quite well, sir," Susan would add. " 'Oh, it's of no consequence, thank'ee,' was the invariable reply of Mr. Toots, and when he had said so, he always went away very fast."

"It's of no consequence." How shockingly irrelevant this sounds in our world of frantic demand for results! It takes courage of a high order to cling to the ultimate truth of Mr. Toots' phrase, and we cannot do it at all unless we deeply care and are prepared to take full responsibility for the consequences of our words and actions on all other levels. Let us look back for a moment at Sybil Coningsby. She never interferes with people or situations, imposing her opinions or her will, yet she never refuses a responsibility. She invariably acts and speaks out of her deep caring. She gravely and courteously answers the mad woman; she saves the terrified kitten; she tends Aaron's sprained ankle; and she goes out into the storm to find her brother, simply because each act is the inevitable response of her whole being to the immediate situation. No responsibility is either too large or too small for her. She knows that the storm may destroy her and them all, but her one concern is to hold inwardly to the joy of The Fool, for whom "It's of no consequence," while acting practically out of the achieved courtesy of her mind and heart. She is the only one who is not trying to produce any final result, good or bad, and therefore the only one who is, in the true sense, totally involved. Therefore, it is, of course, through her that the storm is finally controlled and the conflicts are resolved. It is so easy to forget in these frantic times how much, how very much, may depend on those who can live from that deep level and say, "It's of no consequence."

This may seem a far cry from Mr. Toots, but not so. He, too, is wholly involved and at the same time wholly free with the freedom of The Fool; moreover, he brings us the great saving gift of laughter. How different is his innocence from the unbelievable and sickeningly "good" innocence of Florence, meekly white-washing her father and blaming herself for his cruelties! Mr. Toots never deceives himself in matters of feeling. He can be in transports of delight, deepest gloom, agonies of uncertainty, vi-olent jealousy, heartfelt admiration—and can express each one of these emotions with his whole heart. The descriptions of his reaction when he knows that Florence loves Walter are abso-lutely enchanting. He talks a good deal about the "silent tomb." One moment he can't stand to be in the room with Walter and rushes out; having overcome this emotion, back he comes, seizes Walter by the hand, and wishes him well from the bottom of his guileless heart. We may think that Florence made a bad choice when she preferred the colorless Walter Gay, but then how relieved we are that Mr. Toots ends up married to the alto-gether delightful and pithy Susan Nipper. "The most extraordi-nary woman in the world," says Mr. Toots, and he explains that he has not had to give up his old love or make any pretense about it. For him Florence will always be the most beautiful of her sex; but, he says, Susan, that extraordinary woman, agrees with him! So they are immensely and enduringly happy and we feel that to-gether, like The Fool, they could walk unharmed over preci-pices, for theirs is the final security of "idiot joy" and "idiot love."

Chesterton writes, "The key to the great characters of Dickens is that they are all great fools. There is the same difference be-tween a great fool and a small fool as there is between a great poet and a small poet. The great fool is a being who is above wisdom rather than below it." And of Toots himself he says that Dickens does not gloss over any of his deficiencies but makes them suddenly "like violent virtues that we would go to the world's end to see." Dickens, through such fools as Toots, "makes us lively where we were bored, kind where we were cruel, and above all, free for a universal human laughter where we were cramped in a small competition about that sad and solemn thing, the intellect."

"This largeness," Chesterton continues, "this grossness and gorgeousness of folly is the thing that we all feel about those with whom we are in intimate contact; and it is the one enduring basis of affection and even of respect."[9] Indeed yes! Love that is true and unshakable is born in us when there is also laughter, at each other and with each other at the same moment—the laughter of The Fool of the Tarot—dancing with his tiger in each, with each and between the two, in all our meetings.

I think it very likely that when we arrive at the Pearly Gates we may meet Mr. Toots resplendent in a new and preposterous waistcoat from the heavenly Burgess and Company, and that he will greet us with a rush of embarrassed words, answering his own question as always, "How de do. I'm quite well, thank you. It's of no consequence, you know," and we will then know as we chuckle and choke that truly we have arrived in Heaven.

8

Exchange as the Way of Conscious Love

In three of his works Charles Williams wrote explicitly of that which he called "the practice of substituted love," which was, in his thought and in his life, the conscious and active manifestation of the "coinherence," or "exchange," at the heart of the universe. In the novel *Descent into Hell,* two of the characters consciously practice this substitution, and in the poem "The Founding of the Company" (which is part of his Arthurian cycle), the king's poet becomes the leader of a company of those who are linked together, not by any rule or outer form, but simply by "a certain pointing," a free choice of the way of exchange that is conscious love. C.S. Lewis says of this poem that it is autobiographical as well as mythological, for "something like Taliesin's company probably came into being wherever Charles Williams had lived and worked."[1] The third and theoretical definition of this concept is in one of the chapters of Williams' essay *He Came Down from Heaven.* If we summarize the ideas in this chapter, we shall then perhaps be able to see the ways in which they may operate in our lives.

There are three degrees of consciousness, Williams says: (1) the old self on the old way, (2) the old self on the new way, (3) the new self on the new way. Williams writes:

The second group is the largest at all times and in all places . . . it forms . . . at most moments practically all of oneself that one can know, for the new self does not know itself. It consists of the existence of the self, unselfish perhaps, but not yet denied. This self often applies itself unselfishly. It transfers its activities from itself unselfishly as a centre to its belief as a centre. It uses its angers on behalf of its religion or its morals, and its greed and its fear and its pride. It operates on behalf of its notion of God as it originally operated on behalf of itself. It aims honestly at better behaviour, but it does not usually aim at change.[2]

This change Williams now defines as the birth of a new kind of love: "To love is to die and to live again; to live from a new root. . . . We are to love each other . . . by acts of substitution." "He saved others; Himself he cannot save." This, Williams says, is an "exact definition of the Kingdom of Heaven in operation and of the great discovery of substitution then made by earth."[3]

The maxims of unselfishness are universally preached and, as long as "the old self on the new way" remains, they are perhaps a necessary stage; but the difference between unselfishness and self-denial is very rarely understood. In Jung's language, as long as we are trying to improve the ego by inducing "good" feelings in it or urging it to the performance of "good" works, then we merely succeed in nourishing an equivalent amount of "bad" feeling in the unconscious, which will have negative effects somewhere in our environment. Only when the center of our feeling and action is rooted in the Self instead of the self (ego) can our love and our goodness reach beyond this pendulum swing of the opposites.

The word *self-denial* as used by Williams means exactly this. The denial of the ego does not imply that we are rid of it; it means that it acts only as the agent, so to speak, of the Self, or the "new self on the new way," which has transcended both selfishness and unselfishness by the acceptance of substituted love. "Neither Jew nor Greek, but a new creature." Neither self-sacrifice nor self-gratification as such; both may be sacraments of love at any moment, but neither is covenanted. The denial of the self affects both. "It is no more I that live, but Christ that liveth in me" is the definition of the pure life that is substituted for both.

Williams, who is never content with mere words, now proceeds to a practical definition of how this new love is to be lived. He takes the hackneyed text "Bear ye one another's burdens" and gives it a new dimension, interpreting it as a law of interior self-denial instead of the usual exterior exhortation to unselfishness. How can we literally carry the anxiety, fear, or misery of another? At this point we should be warned that the actual person-to-person exchange of burdens described so vividly, especially in *Descent into Hell,* would be a dangerous and unreal thing for most of us if we self-consciously copied the technique. Nevertheless, something like it does actually come about in those who have chosen to follow the way of individuation, of "self-denial" as defined above. To understand another's technique can lead either to literal copying, which is worse than useless, or to more light on our own way.

In the poem, Taliesin's company has three degrees. In the first degree are those who live by "a frankness of honorable exchange" on the outer level.[4] C.S. Lewis, speaking of these, calls them "those . . . who willingly and honorably and happily maintain the complex system of exchanged services on which society depends. There is nothing to distinguish them from people outside the Company except the fact that they do consciously and joyously, and therefore excellently what everyone save parasites has to do in some fashion."[5]

In the second degree are those who practice substitution, as Williams defined it, by bearing consciously a particular interior burden for another person. To do this there are three necessities. The burden must first be fully known; secondly, it must be freely given up by the one; and thirdly, it must be consciously taken up by the other. In *Descent into Hell* these three points are seen in action. Pauline has first to find the courage to tell Stanhope of her fear, which sounds ridiculous and of which she is ashamed; she then has to consent to his carrying it and to letting go of it herself. Stanhope must offer to carry it, opening himself in imagination to all that she is experiencing but without personal, emotional involvement. The result is not the release of Pauline from the necessity of facing her problem but the lifting from her of the personal terror that had literally forced her into a continual running away. The "new self," however, is not fully born in her until she, in her turn, is willing to carry the suffering of another. Sometimes, Williams says, it is a reciprocal exchange between two individuals; more often it is a chain—you carry my burden; I carry someone else's.

We may try now to translate these three points into terms of our own experience. Substitution is a fact of the psyche and will take place either through the mechanism of projections, forcing others to carry bits of ourselves, or by sucking strength from them via the unconscious; or it can become a conscious exchange of love in the way that Williams describes. First, then, there is the necessity for an absolutely honest speaking out of our problem, our misery, to another person whose offer of himself we recognize and accept. This is no easy thing, but we all know that without it no change of any kind, let alone exchange and substitution, can even begin. It is simple to go to someone and complain of our problems, leaving out the essential facts, but that is an entirely sterile proceeding. In fact, the second necessity, the willingness to give up the fear or the grief or the anxiety, is easily recognizable in the manner in which the suffering is expressed. As long as there is any trace of self-pity, there is no hope at all that the burden can be lifted by another, nor if there is any dramatization or implication of "hard luck" or of throwing the blame upon another. "Self-denial" is as necessary for the sufferer as for the one who offers to help. Williams says, "It is habitual with us to prefer to be miserable rather than to give and to believe that we can give our miseries up."[6]

To give up a pleasure is not so difficult because it is easy simply to replace it with a still more pleasurable feeling of being noble and self-sacrificing; but to give up a misery (truly to let go of it, not just replace it temporarily with an evasion) is to deprive the ego of one of its major sources of nourishment. The ego, taking its problem to another, is merely making a bid for attention, trying to involve the other emotionally; and to build up a sense of significance that covers the inner bankruptcy of the "old self." In order to feel meaningful, the old self must always be either dramatically weak and miserable, or dramatically strong and unselfish, busily helping the weak and miserable and deciding what is right for them. The two attitudes are often there together, compensating each other in a futile waste of energy. The "new self," on the other hand, will, when in misery, ask for help with simple acceptance and willingness to let go no matter how empty he may feel; or, if he is the taker of the burden, he will give of himself without any sense of being thereby increased in significance. The "old self" can only be thrust into another swing of the pendulum. There is no real healing. It must be emphasized again that the relief of the sufferer in no way implies that he is saved from the necessity to meet his problem, to face the facts, but only that the terror or anxiety that has sapped his strength is lifted from him.

The taker of the burden must consciously take it up, says Williams, by imagining, feeling himself into the fear or pain of the other. For us to say, even to ourselves, "Now I am going to carry this person's burden for him" would be very dangerous because almost certainly we would find ourselves on the wrong level, caught by the old self and unconsciously building up a sense of power and importance. Only he who is completely rooted in the Self, the new "self," can use this language safely. We have to be constantly on the watch for emotional dramas in the unconscious that feed our greed for giving (a specifically feminine trait), just as easily as they nourish our greed for taking. The former is the more dangerous because it looks good. The conscious taking of the burden is for us rather the meeting of any request for help on any level, outer or inner, with a high degree of awareness, both of feeling and intelligence. It is very difficult indeed not to respond either with a rush of identifying emotion—"I can't stand to see this person suffer. I must make him feel better"—or else with some kind of evasion based on a fear of our own. We have to open ourselves to the impact of another's suffering, *not* on the level of emotional involvement but through real feeling, which always involves intelligent discrimination. So there must be the clear refusal to accept a mere bid for attention, or to respond to self-pity or false emotionalism in the other, and only then may we use all the powers of the imagination to understand and the strength of our perception of the "new self" to relieve the suffering of another. In this kind of meeting between two people there may superficially seem to be one who helps and another who is helped, but in the moment of truth between them there is no such distinction—each is helper and helped in the same moment and in each there is a new birth of consciousness.

Any other kind of "helping others" is psychic trespassing. Surely "Forgive us our trespasses" may be said to apply with especial intensity to this urge to solve the problems of others who have not asked in any real way for help, or who, having asked, are only looking for a bolstering up of the "old self." If we become aware of such an urge or drive in ourselves, so different from a simple openness to any real need that is brought to us (and this is a highly active state of consciousness, not just a passive drifting), then we may be sure that we are evading some fear of insignificance, some misery of our own that we are not willing to know and to give up. Indeed, the only safe and sure way for us is to concentrate on the exceedingly difficult task of knowing our own misery and letting it go, because only to the extent that we attain to this shall we be in the state of consciousness that bears another's burden. It will come to us inevitably without any seeking, as a necessity of the way.

There is likewise a need for intelligence in the meeting even of real requests for help of any kind. Williams insists on this at some length. Before offering our help, outer or inner, we are obligated to weigh the extent of our available energy and whether the taking of a new burden would be to the detriment of other values or other people in our lives. This kind of discrimination can be very difficult, as we well know. There is a beautiful passage toward the end of *He Came Down from Heaven*; "The new earth and the new heaven come like the two modes of knowledge, knowledge being the chief art of love, as love is the chief art of knowledge."[7] Love without intelligence is formless emotion, and intelligence without love an empty sterility.

The third degree in the company is something, as C.S. Lewis says, much harder to understand except for those few who have achieved it. It can come only when the "new self" is fully realized—in Jung's language, when the Self has finally replaced the ego at the center of life—or, in the words of St. Paul, "I live, yet not I, but Christ liveth in me." We may conclude that these few experience, beyond all individual substitution, the total coherence of all things at all times and in all places.

9

Inner Relationship and Community in the I Ching

The wisdom of the *I Ching,* the Book of Changes, speaks to us across the three thousand years of its life in a language that, though strange to us at first, has an extraordinarily modern accent.[1] This is not the occasion for a detailed explanation of the structure of the book and for our purpose it is enough to say that it contains sixty-four so-called "signs" or "hexagrams," representing different combinations of the masculine and feminine principles, the "yang" and the "yin" aspects of life, each hexagram giving wisdom for a particular situation of human life in time.

A hexagram is composed of six lines, unbroken masculine and feminine lines, and each of these lines refers to a special aspect of the time situation symbolized by the particular sign. Each hexagram begins with a "judgment" and an "image," the first describing the basic meaning of the whole sign, the second expressing another aspect of it in imagery. Thus the clarity of conscious judgment and the symbolism of the unconscious meet and illuminate each other throughout the book.

There are a number of hexagrams that deal specifically with different kinds of relatedness. They include: The Family, Fellowship with Men, The Marrying Maiden, Holding Together, Gathering Together, Influence, Inner Truth. We shall quote from these and discuss some of the wisdom they contain.

We begin with the natural group of the family (Hexagram 37). The basic teaching of this sign lays down at once an unchanging essential for any kind of real relatedness between people at any level. There must be boundaries, separateness; each individual must be distinct, and there must be discrimination of function. In the Judgment it is said, "If the father is really a father and the son a son—if the husband is really a husband and the wife a wife, then the family is in order." How well we know in our day that the breakdown of the family comes from the loss of this wisdom! We see on all sides the woman behaving unconsciously like a man, the man a prey to feminine moods and softness, the child treated like an adult, or parents descending to childish behavior, and all the resulting misery and disorder of the indiscriminate mixture of function.

Of the six lines of the hexagram, one speaks of the child, one of woman and child, two of woman, and two of man. For the child the essential is that there should be rules of order that he may recognize from the very beginning and within which he may be entirely free. Freedom without such basic rules is a terrible burden to lay on a child. "When tempers flare up in the family, too great severity brings remorse, good fortune nonetheless. When woman and child dally and laugh, it leads in the end to humiliation." Even if we make occasional mistakes, it is better to have too much discipline than to descend to the child's level. We need to "build strong dykes" within which each individual (not only the child) can move freely, but one small hole in a dyke can let in a flood.

To the woman the *I Ching* speaks in this sign with especial force. "It is upon the woman of the house that the well-being of the family depends." "The atmosphere that holds the family together" depends on the woman, for she is the heart of the house, the one who nourishes it both outwardly and inwardly. "She should not follow her whims. She must attend within to the food." "She must attend to the nourishment of her family and to the food for the sacrifice. In this way she becomes the center of the social and religious life of the family. . . ." In our language, it is the feminine principle that binds people together, the "cement" in all relationships, and this binding force of the heart may either bring people together in a true meeting or turn into the destructive and imprisoning possessiveness of the woman who follows her whim; that is to say, whose feeling consists of unconscious emotional drives instead of conscious discrimination and warmth. It is the woman, or the *anima* in a man, who maintains the link with the depths of the unconscious, the springs of the religious instinct in man. Hence, she provides "the food for the sacrifice."

On the father of the family the *I Ching* urges the cultivation of his own personality so that he may carry his responsibility freely and willingly and exercise authority through trustworthiness and love, never through fear. If his character is centered on inner truth, his influence in the family will operate for its wellbeing without conscious contriving.

"The Family is society in embryo," says the *I Ching*. In every sign there are different levels of interpretation—the personal, the social and political, the cosmic; and we today may add another, the interpretation of these signs as inner situations of the individual psyche. In this particular hexagram, the advice as to discrimination of function, for instance, is profoundly valid as applied to the different aspects of a single personality. We need to be aware of the child in us, to give him or her discipline and freedom; the feminine parts of our nature, whether we be men or women, must attend to the "food" and beware of "whims"; the masculine authority must be realized through objective love and not through fear; and so on. We have not evolved any better advice in 3,000 years.

We move out from containment in the family to seek "Fellowship with men"(Hexagram 13). Here the necessity for discrimination, for "distinction between things" is again stressed. "Fellowship should not be a mere mingling of individuals or of things—that would be chaos not fellowship." The lines speak of the most dangerous pitfalls. "Fellowship with men in the clan brings humiliation." There is danger here of the formation of a separate function on the basis of personal and egotistic motives." Any kind of exclusive feeling must wreck real fellowship, and is something entirely different from separateness and observance of boundaries between men.

The next line warns against mistrust and suspicion. If we have mental reservations, if there is a conscious or unconscious holding back, or refusal to give of ourselves, then we will always be suspecting the same wiles in others and "the result is that one departs further and further from true fellowship." Interpreting this inwardly we know that mistrust of ourselves is the root of all suspicion. "We condemn one group in order to unite with others"; that is, we want to accept the parts of ourselves that we like and esteem, and to reject those impulses and weaknesses which make us feel small or guilty. This rejection we project outward into condemnation of other people, feelings of superiority, or into protestations of our inferiority and worthlessness. We are thus incapable of fellowship.

"The Marrying Maiden"(Hexagram 54) speaks of close personal relationships based on affection.

> Affection as the essential principle of relatedness is of the greatest importance in all relationships in the world. . . . Affection is the all-inclusive principle of union. . . . But every relationship between individuals bears within it the danger that wrong turns may be taken leading to endless misunderstandings and disagreements. . . . Therefore, it is necessary constantly to remain mindful of the end. If we permit ourselves to drift along, we come together and are parted again as the day may determine.

We must "understand the transitory in the light of the eternity of the end." In other words, if our love for another person becomes an end in itself, shutting out all other loves, breeding jealousy and exclusiveness, it is not real love at all. It is by no means easy to remain "mindful of this end," of that which is beyond the personal, when we are seized by an overmastering longing for another person's love. The top line of the hexagram stresses the absolute necessity for "sacrifice" in the real sense of the word, if love is to endure. If "the woman holds the basket but there are no fruits in it," or "the man stabs the sheep, but no blood flows," then affection and love will turn in the long run to hate. The meaning of this image is that in the Chinese rite of sacrifice to the ancestors the woman presented harvest offerings, while the man slaughtered the sacrificial animal. We should say that the woman must sacrifice her possessiveness, must offer her "fruits," let go of her children, her *demand* to be loved, while a man must sacrifice his aggressive instincts, his sensuality in its blind, unfeeling form.

We come now to the hexagram that deals specifically with the coming together of men in communities or groups. The *I Ching* points out that there is in man a need for relationship in groups as well as between individuals. In our day, owing to the breakdown of the traditional family, social, and religious values, and still more because of the split between intellect and instinct, between conscious and unconscious, in the collective psyche, this need has become almost frenzied. "Togetherness," that frightening word, has replaced relationship, and has become a cultural ideal. Study groups, conferences, camps, "workshops," human "laboratories," spring up on every side to meet a very real human need, but they have also their danger. Often designed to help people toward self-knowledge, they become for many a protection against that very thing, a running away from the essentially lonely tasks of facing the dark sides of the individual soul. Therefore, very great care and awareness is needed before one joins any kind of group. Will this mean running away for me one must ask, or will it bring real support and new consciousness? The essential inner journey must be made alone, but all of us need support and relatedness with others of like mind; and it is fatally easy to mistake dependence, a blind acceptance of the opinions of others, for real mutual support, for the humility that respects another's view but never swallows it whole. Men desperately fly from loneliness to "togetherness," but the only real cure for loneliness is to accept the "aloneness" of the spirit, and then, to our astonishment, real relatedness, real friendship, will come to our doorstep, wherever we may be.

The *I Ching* says of itself that it speaks only to the "superior" man, which in our language means the "conscious" man, and the wisdom of "Holding Together"(Hexagram 8) and "Gathering Together"(Hexagram 45) would mean little to those who seek community for escapist reasons. It speaks to those who seek a holding together with others of like mind as free individuals, to those who are striving for the wholeness that Jung has called "individuation."

Both hexagrams begin by emphasizing the necessity for a leader, a person around whom others unite. The ancient Chinese culture was feudal, but the validity of the principle remains. The elected representative in a democracy must take up and carry the responsibility of leadership for his term of office, but he is protected as far as is collectively possible from identifying personally with his power. In every kind of group, even that which is a gathering of free and conscious individuals, there must be leadership—the kind about which Charles Williams wrote so beautifully when he described the "excellent absurdity" of one man acting as a center for others. He must at all times be aware of his ultimate unimportance and dispensability, must be wholly aware that he is not the center, but merely a focal point through which, if this task has been laid upon him, others may recognize *the* center within themselves. In this Charles Williams is entirely at one with the teaching of the *I Ching*.

In the commentary on one of the lines in the sign "Holding Together," it is said of the leader: "Those who come to him he accepts, those who do not come are allowed to go their own way. He invites none, flatters none—all come of their own free will. In this way there develops a voluntary dependence among those who hold to him. They do not have to be constantly on their guard but may express their opinions openly. Police measures are not necessary. The same principle is valid for life in general. We should not woo favor from people. If a man cultivates within himself the purity and strength that are necessary for one who is the center of a fellowship, those who are meant for him come of their own accord."

If there is this kind of freedom in a community, then each member of it will begin to find real leadership within himself, the impersonal purity and strength, the center, the "Self" displacing the ego's leadership. Around this center first of all his own personality will "gather," and it will then be felt by all those who are "meant for him." "A leader must be collected within himself."

In another hexagram called "Following," it is said that all those who are followed must themselves know how to follow. When the situation requires any one of us to lead, we must have the courage and humility to do so, and when it is time to be led, this also we accept in freedom and true independence. The one requires the other; indeed, they beget each other.

The first line in the sign "Holding Together" speaks of the fundamental sincerity that is the essential for all relationship. "This attitude, symbolized by a full earthen bowl, in which the content is everything and the empty form nothing, shows itself not in clever words but through the strength of what lies within the speaker." The second line points out that if we are seeking any kind of personal advantage from our association with a group, then we "lose ourselves." In other words, we are merely bolstering up unconscious demands; we are not individuals anymore.

The third line reads, "You hold together with the wrong people." This is a warning against false intimacy with people who do not meet us on our own deepest level. This does not mean that we may not enjoy the company of such people, but the commentary insists with surprising force on the danger of *inti-*

macy in the wrong place. "We must beware of being drawn into false intimacy through force of habit. Maintaining sociability without intimacy is the only right attitude—because otherwise we should not be free to enter into relationship with people of our own kind." In our terms, to reveal ourselves, our thoughts and feelings to someone who does not understand our basic values is not only pointless—it exposes us to invasion by superficial attitudes and literally corrupts or steals away our energy, dissipating it, or imprisoning it, so that we have nothing left to give to the true relationship.

Another line warns against too long a delay in giving "complete and full devotion" to the group that we have recognized to be the carrier of our real values. The hexagram is concerned with groups, but we may interpret this line as also warning of those moments when we are capable of a new and more complete commitment to the way of individuation, moments when we have to make a vital choice. "If we have missed the right moment for union and go on hesitating to give complete and full devotion, we shall regret the error when it is too late." A dream will often bring to consciousness this necessity for a choice and if we refuse it, it may be a long time before the opportunity returns.

The hexagram of "Gathering Together" is very similar to that of "Holding Together," but it deals with one other aspect of the subject—the danger of strife and conflict within a group and of "robbery" from without. The *I Ching* says that there is one strong defense against these splitting attacks from within and from without—a constant watchfulness and foresight. We must *expect* these things. "Human woes usually come as a result of unexpected events against which we are not forearmed." We are continually thrown by our own moods and weaknesses into destructive attitudes, because, when things are going well, we cease to expect any setback, and when it comes, we fall into discouragement and seek for scapegoats. In the first line we are told what to do in such a case. "If you are sincere but not to the end, there will sometimes be confusion, sometimes gathering together. If you call out, then after one grasp of the hand you can laugh again. Regret not."

A beautiful passage from the commentary on another line may end our study of these two signs.

> In the time of gathering together we should make no arbitrary choice of the way. There are secret forces at work leading to-

gether those that belong together. We must yield to this attraction; then we make no mistakes. Where inner relationships exist, no great preparations and formalities are necessary. People understand one another forthwith, just as the Divinity accepts a small offering if it comes from the heart.

There is a passage in *Man and His Symbols* in the section by Marie Louise von Franz that sums up this wisdom in modern terms:

> It is ultimately the Self that orders and regulates one's human relationships, so long as the conscious ego takes the trouble to detect the delusive projections and deals with these inside himself instead of outside. It is in this way that spiritually attuned and similarly oriented people find their way to one another, to create a group that cuts across all the usual social and organizational affiliations of people. Such a group is not in conflict with others; it is merely different and independent. The consciously realized process of individuation thus changes a person's relationships. The familiar bonds such as kinship or common interests are replaced by a different type of unity—a bond through the Self.[2]

In the sign "Dispersion" or "Dissolution"(Hexagram 59) the necessity for dissolving these old familiar bonds to collective groups is stressed, so that the new and free type of union may be born. "He dissolves his bond with his group. Supreme good fortune. Dispersion leads in turn to accumulation. This is something that ordinary men do not think of." In another sign (Decrease 41) there is a line, "When three people journey together their number decreases by one, but where one man journeys alone, he finds a companion." Only when a man can stand alone does he find the real unity with others.

"Influence"(Hexagram 31) is concerned with the ways in which one may safely influence others or be influenced by them. The image for this sign is a mountain with a sunken peak holding the water of a lake. The mountain in the *I Ching* is the symbol of keeping still; the lake stands for joy. If we know how to keep still inwardly, others may be nourished by our joy and we will be receptive to any true influence from without. The lines point out some of the pitfalls. "If a man runs precipitately after everyone he would like to influence or yields immediately and without thought to every whim of those he would like to please, then the result is inevitably humiliation.'' The most superficial of all ways of trying to influence others is through talk with nothing real behind it, mere tonguewagging. However,

> when the quiet power of a man's own character is at work, the effects produced are right. All those who are receptive to the vibrations of such a spirit will then be influenced. Influence over others should not express itself as a conscious and willed effort to manipulate them. Through practicing such conscious incitement, one becomes wrought up and is exhausted by the eternal stress and strain. Moreover, the effects produced are then limited to those on whom one's thoughts are consciously fixed.

Finally in the hexagram of ''Inner Truth''(61) there is a line that most beautifully expresses this deepest level of all in the relationship of one man with another. The text is ''A crane calling in the shade. Its young answer it. I have a good goblet. I will share it with you.''
And the commentary:

> This refers to the involuntary influence of a man's inner being upon persons of kindred spirit. The crane may be quite hidden when it sounds its call. Where there is a joyous mood, there a comrade will appear to share a glass of wine. Whenever a feeling is voiced with truth and frankness, whenever a deed is the clear expression of sentiment, a mysterious and far-reaching influence is exerted. At first it acts on those who are inwardly receptive. But the circle grows larger and larger. The root of all influence lies in one's inner being. . . . Any deliberate intention of an effect would only destroy the possibility of producing it.

Confucius said about this line:

> The superior man abides in his room. If his words are well spoken, he meets with assent at a distance of more than a thousand miles. How much more then from nearby! If the superior man abides in his room and his words are not well spoken, he meets with contradiction at a distance of more than a thousand miles. How much more, then, from nearby! Through words and deeds the superior man moves heaven and earth. Must one not, then, be cautious?

10

Pride

I once heard a dream in which there was the image of a man who had lived fully and deeply, passing through many experiences to maturity. A voice spoke in the dream and said of him: "He has learned the pride of the lion; he must now learn the pride of the unicorn."

Pride is a word almost always used negatively, but it has another and more positive meaning. A proud man in this sense is one who will not behave in a manner which degrades or does not benefit his essential nature—one who does not allow himself to act out of a standard of values less noble, less conscious, than his best. To the extent that a man identifies value with his ego qualities and desires he falls into the deadly sin of personal pride. His pride is then comparative: "I am better, or worse, than someone else." But that other pride is never comparative. It is simply that which refuses to compromise with the second best, and it contains no thought of self-justification or false apology.

The word "proud" comes from the old French word *prut* which later became *preux*. A *preux chevalier* was one who was always true to the meaning of his knighthood—not proud *of himself,* but incorruptible in his loyalty to the values of chivalry, to the courage, courtesy, and selflessness which were the code of the knight. The one who betrayed these things and fought dishonourably for base ends to serve his own ego would never have been called *preux.*

It is not for nothing that we speak of a "pride of lions," for those old collective words expressed very often a salient quality in the beasts or birds they described. The lion is felt by man to be a king among beasts. His pride is very different from the human sin of usurping a merit not his own; it is a natural pride which is the quality of being true to oneself. A lion who turns man-eating, when unable through injury to catch his natural prey, becomes a lion outlaw and is cast out of his pride, for he is untrue to his lion nature, no longer a proud king amongst beasts. It is interesting to remember how Laurens van der Post writes of the Bushman's feeling for the lion.[1] He also says that the lion is far and away the most individual of the wild animals in Africa. Every lion you encounter will act in a different way and you can never predict his behaviour as you can with almost all the other species. This is reflected in the beautiful Bushman story of how the lion singled out a man and forced him finally into coming out from behind the protection of his tribe, into taking responsibility for his own decisions.

This, then, is how a man learns the "pride" of the lion. He must emerge from the protection of convention and from dependence on collective authority and enter into life with the courage both to kill and be killed, as it were, a thousand times, as a lion must kill to eat and risk the guns of the hunters. For once we have experienced the Fall and innocence is lost, we are plunged into the battle of the opposites, and we can never be involved in this battle as anything but unconscious pawns until we have learned that we must, symbolically speaking, kill in order to eat, and be killed that others may eat. "The pride of the lion" in this context, then, is that which comes to the man who consciously accepts this symbolic truth, and the suffering it brings. Thus he emerges from the meaningless state of tearing others to pieces and being torn in the *unconscious,* which is so often the condition of those who preach universal good will and a bloodless kind of psychic pacifism. We have only to think of what would happen if all fighting and killing were to be expunged from the great myths of the world to realize that life would be meaningless without fighting. The long journey toward consciousness involves constant and ruthless fighting and killing; primitive man would have starved without it, and a man in any age who tries to evade it on all levels is still sucking milk from his mother's breast in a state of arrested development. Any kind of pacifism that refuses *all* fighting and killing is not only doomed to failure, since it denies validity to one of the basic facts of the unconscious, but it actually breeds more and more violence, violence of an unconscious kind which kills in order to feed those hideous distortions of human nature—the pride of the ego, its power and its greed. To be released from this kind of violence we have to accept the necessity of fighting with every ounce of our strength, but *on an inner not an outer battlefield.* It is even, I believe, true that, as long as men are unable to fight and to kill and expose themselves to be killed in their inner world, then it is a great deal better that they find the meaning of courage and self-sacrifice on some form of outer battlefield with all its horror than that they live out their lives in a simulation of peace under which they spread destruction through the unconscious into the lives of their neighbours.

Man's urge to stir up war has increasingly through the centuries been generated by his boredom. He has an absolute need to fight obstacles, to "kill the dragon," to know in himself the heroic devotion which proves him a man—and, the fewer the natural obstacles in life, the greater his need for *either* an outer or an inner battlefield. That is the choice. Until there are enough individuals who find and fight their inner battles, wars must continue, and the horrible thing is that war today is becoming more and more a thing of the head, and we are in danger of wars in which the ordinary man is not involved with heart and body at all except as a target. Rockets and bombs, aimed by scientific means from great distances, germ warfare and so on, are violence absolutely stripped of all its potential cathartic meaning— the cold violence of pure barbarity from which all values of devotion and sacrifice have been eliminated.

So it becomes more and more imperative that we dare to fight in our own personal lives; and it is a great deal better that we fight openly and outwardly the people around us when it is a matter of standing by our essential values, however immature these values may be, than that we hide behind a pacifistic pseudo-harmony, and then go about spreading hostility and bad feeling in an indirect manner. As long as we are split and the opposites hold sway we will do as much harm to others in our lives as good, as indeed Jung said once of himself. We may, however, think of the immense debt we owe to those who have dealt us mortal blows in the course of our lives, thus revealing to us our own truth and, while it does not relieve us of our guilt for our own unconscious killing, we still may know that perhaps our darkness has brought light to others.

Some pacifists hold that a man is almost as guilty of killing another man in war as he is if he kills for some personal end. But the practically universal judgment of mankind of this issue does not err, and the distinction is absolutely valid in the personal world. If a man fight out of his devotion to something, a value, a feeling beyond his ego's pride and desire, if he kills out of *need,* whether it be the killing of animals for food, or of men when an essential value is threatened, he is not as guilty as he is guilty if he kills out of greed and hatred. It is here that the natural "kill and be killed" of the animal world brings us a basic lesson. In an Indian story the lion brought up with goats and refusing to eat game is shown as an offense against nature—a shocking, ugly thing. We are not animals, and for us to live out the animal side of our nature without thought and moral judgment is equally an offense against the nature of man. Jung repeated may times that a man—if he is to be true to his humanity—must live by an ethic which every person who seeks individuation must find for himself. When we have accepted both these things, the animal and the ethical, and are willing to kill and be killed, if necessary, in the service of our deeply felt values, then we have learned "the pride of the lion." Christ said of himself, "I am come not to bring peace but a sword" (Matt. 10:34).

The pride of the lion, however, is far from being the end. There comes a time when this pride must in its turn be abandoned, transmuted into the pride of the unicorn; and if a man refuses this sacrifice and the quest of the "unicorn" when the time is ripe, he will surely fall back again into a worse and more deadly state of personal pride.

When the pride of the unicorn is born in a man he has no more need to fight, for he has begun to find his nourishment through that love which is beyond the love-hate opposites. The unicorn does not kill; he harms nothing. His horn is uplifted in a remote and lovely pride as we glimpse him now and then on his swift course. Yet like all true pride it is humble. The power of his horn comes to rest on the lap of the virgin (the ancient meaning of the word "virgin" was "she who is one-in-herself"), and here he gives himself willingly to the knife of the hunter. The sage, the holy one, the Boddhisattva, who *chooses* to remain in this world, as it is said in the East, has reached the stage where no hurt of any kind goes out from him. Nevertheless, being here in the world of opposites, he is not freed from their effects. Consciously, willingly, he exposes himself to the hatred of the world, not in a weak and watery pacifism, but having fought the bitter and bloody battle entirely within himself through repeated sacrifice.

Frodo, at the end of *The Lord of the Rings,* is an image of this. At their return to the Shire after the defeat of the Dark Lord, the Hobbits had to fight to clear the land of the evil that had crept in in their absence. For Merry and Pippin and Sam this was an inevitable duty, "lions" as they were, in spite of the killing it involved. But Frodo had become a "unicorn." He could never draw sword again, though he accepted with sorrow that it must be so for others. No hurt went out from him, though for the brief time that remained before he "went into the West," he suffered still from the wounds that he had taken in the days of his fight with the dark powers.

Surely we glimpse and faintly experience the pride of the unicorn every time we succeed in detaching for a moment from the battle of the opposites, repressing neither the one side nor the other, accepting both—a thing which can only be done through the intense imaginative experience of a uniting symbol. When our feelings are hurt, or we are angry or depressed, if we make the effort to objectify the emotion, not rationally but through active imagination in some form or other, and so give it validity as separate from the ego, we are able to accept conscious responsibility for it as part of the suffering of all humanity. Thus a little bit of our ego's pride is sacrificed at the feet of the "virgin," and for that instant no harm goes out from us into the world as we touch the final innocence.

Only by entering through imaginative vision into the sacrificial death can we come to the transition from the pride of the lion to the pride of the unicorn. Man has known this intuitively from the very beginning, as all the great myths show.

The very first incident after the Fall proclaims it. Abel offered a blood sacrifice to God, symbol of the longing to sanctify the instinct to kill and so to return to the wholeness of innocence, but Cain, the shadow brother, will have none of this. His pride is comparative—"God loves Abel better than he loves me." So he kills his brother—the first murder. And yet, as is hinted in God's protection of Cain, this killing had to be. Mankind *had* to plunge into the split, had to experience the ego's pride, to fight and to kill, and to take the long way through projection and the endless sacrifices by which it is withdrawn, before he could return to innocence. An angel with a flaming sword guarded the backward way into Eden. So every adolescent must learn to fight for his life, must find first the ego and its pride, then the pride of the lion, until, if his courage holds, he may come finally to know the pride of the unicorn, laying down his strength in the virgin's lap.

The book of Job is the story of a man's passing from the pride of the lion to the pride of the unicorn. "Though he slay me, yet will I trust in Him. But I will maintain my ways before him. My righteousness I hold fast and I will not let it go" (Job 13:15). That is a glorious pride before the onslaught of God. And God commended it, as opposed to the false modesty of Job's friends, insisting on guilt and retribution. It was, however, time for Job to go beyond this pride of the lion, this brave assertion of his faith in himself. It was time for him to know the meaning of suffering, not as a consequence of guilt, but as God himself knew it in Christ—as that through which, accepted by the *innocent,* brings the end of the split. "I have heard of thee by the hearing of the ear but now mine eye seeth thee" (Job 42:5). What could be a prouder cry than that coming from the depths of his humble repentance. He had come to the pride of the unicorn, the pride of the clear vision of the whole.

Finally, here is an incident from Helen Waddell's book, *Peter Abelard.* Abelard had been indeed a lion. He had been true to the love of his heart, true to the immense powers of his mind in the teeth of all the violence of collective morality and of the dogmatic narrowness of the church. His reward had been the horrible suffering of physical castration, and the public burning of the book into which he had poured his deepest faith. He was another Job, refusing to pretend to a guilt he did not feel, crying out upon the injustice of God. He shunned men and went to live alone in the woods with Thibault, a young pupil who adored him. Helen Waddell describes how he came to the end of that which I have called the pride of the lion, and to the birth of the unicorn within.

On the feast of All Saints Abelard came alone to the porch of a little country church. He felt shut out, abandoned by God and man. The words of the liturgy floated out to him. "The soul of the just are in the hands of God and the torment of malice hath not touched them. In the sight of the unwise they seemed to die; but they are in *peace.*" He rose and went quickly out of the porch and past the quiet graves. The torment of malice had touched him; the hand of God was not for him.

Then he halted and felt that at last he was alone, face to face with God. "He asked for no pity, he asked for justice, the justice that a man would give his fellow."

"And standing there, braced against Heaven, that wind that had blown upon him once and been forgotten breathed upon him again. It came without observation, for the Kingdom of God is within . . ."

"He saw no heavens opened; he saw no Son of Man. For a moment it seemed to him that all the vital forces in his body were withdrawing themselves, that the sight had left his eyes and the blood was ebbing from his heart: he felt the grey breath of dissolution, the falling asunder of body and soul. For a moment: then his spirit leapt toward heaven in naked adoration. Stripped of all human emotion, with no warmth of contrition, with no passion of devotion, but with every power of his mind, and with every pulse of his body, he worshipped God."

Abelard now walked mile after mile through the November day, and as he walked his past life returned to him and he saw himself as never before. "Every sentence that he had written stood out before him, that glorious array of embattled spears, his strong chivalry of all the powers of the soul . . . fighting for the conquest of the spirit's Palestine, for the worship of the Father in spirit and in truth. But for whom was the glory of that warfare? He had fought against ignorance, against spiritual sloth, against an easy faith that was the faith of gulls and not of men. He had written for his young men, challenging them to doubt, arming them against the deadlier sin of dullness: but did dullness keep a man more insensitive to God than pride?"

He had written beautifully about humility but his heart had swelled as he had written it. "He had strutted like a beadle in a cathedral procession, forgetting that behind him came the Host . . ."

". . . Through what sore discipline of body and soul, through what crucifixion of his pride must he still go before he saw the Kingdom of God? For a moment his flesh and his heart failed. Then he raised his head and began walking steadily towards home. He was chanting as he walked the words that had held for him the torment of all longing and now were forever his. 'The souls of the just are in the hands of God and the torment of malice hath not touched them. In the sight of the unwise they seemed to die; but they are in peace.' "

11

Suffering

"Suffering" is a word used to express so many different kinds of experience that its precision of mean-
ing has been lost. The Latin verb *ferre* means "to bear," "to carry,"
and "suffer" derives from it, with the prefix *sub* meaning "under."
This is reminiscent of the tern "undercarriage"—that which bears
the weight of a vehicle above the wheels—which is an apt image of
the meaning of suffering in human life.

In contrast to the word "suffer," such terms as "affliction,"
"grief," and "depression" all bring images of weight bearing
down. To be afflicted is to be struck down by a blow (*fligere:* to
strike). "Grief" is derived from *gravare,* and to be depressed is
to be pressed down. Only when we suffer in the full sense of the
word do we *carry* the weight. A man may say, "I am so terribly
depressed, I can't bear the suffering," when in fact he may not
be suffering at all, but simply lying down under the weight of
outer circumstances or inner mood.

There are, then, two kinds of experiences which we call suffering: that which is totally unproductive, the neurotic state of
meaningless depression, and that which is the essential condition of every step on the way to that which C.G. Jung has called
individuation. Perhaps these images of weight under which we
fall and lie in self-pity, or of weight which we carry in full consciousness, may be a guideline in moments of darkness. The
blows of great affliction or grief are comparatively rare, but day-
to-day onslaughts of hurt feelings, black moods, exhaustion, re-

sentment, and, most of all, false guilt, are the training ground, and nothing is too small to offer us an opportunity to choose between suffering and depression.

Deeply ingrained in the infantile psyche is the conscious or unconscious assumption that the cure for depression is to replace it with pleasant, happy feelings, whereas the only valid cure for any kind of depression lies in the acceptance of real suffering. To climb out of it in any other way is simply a palliative laying the foundations for the next depression. Nothing whatever has happened to the soul. The roots of all our neuroses lie here, in the conflict between the longing for growth and freedom and our incapacity or refusal to pay the price in suffering of the kind which challenges the supremacy of the ego's demands. This is the crux of the matter (and we may pause here to recognize the exact meaning of the word "crux"). The worst agonies of neurotic misery are endured by the ego rather than a moment of consent to the death of even a small part of its demand or its sense of importance.

We can do something towards tracking down some of the continual evasions of the ego by uncovering our fear of humiliation. From this fear of degradation in our own eyes or in the eyes of others, real or imagined, comes a dead weight of moods and depression. For the truly humble person no humiliation exists. It is impossible to humiliate him or for him to feel humiliation, for "grades" and prestige, questions of his own merit or demerit, have no more meaning for him. But the way to humility lies through the pain of accepted humiliation. In the moment of picking it up and carrying it without any movement towards self-justification we cease to be humiliated and begin to suffer. In this context it is well to realize the extent to which we are all open in the unconscious to the present collective worship of what we may call "grades."

Worship is not too strong a word. The more the conscious ideal of the equality of man is proclaimed on the wrong levels, the more desperate becomes the unconscious urge to assert difference, and the yearning for prestige of all kinds breaks loose from the natural hierarchies of being into the struggles of the ego for ascendancy. The inequalities of class in the aristocratic age, absurd though we may call them, were certainly less conducive to neurosis than the gradings of money, academic prowess, I.Q.'s, and A's, B's, and C's in every department of life, which can so dominate our personal unconscious that we are busy grading our weaknesses day in and day out—a very different thing from searching them out and carrying them. The poison of false values thus invades every corner of the psyche. A question to be constantly asked in moods of weakness and depression is, "Am I grading myself or am I recognizing the golden opportunity to suffer and so to deny to some small degree the ego's demands for prestige?"

The worst stumbling block of all derives from this grading. There was no guilt involved in being born into this or that social class, but nowadays we are beset on every side by false guilt which is inverted pride. If we do not rate a B or at least a C in every department of life, then we deem ourselves guilty. The puritanical strain in our heritage reinforces this until we can even allow our work on our inner life to engender a false sense of guilt about our physical, as well as our emotional weaknesses.

Of course on one level it is true that any kind of symptom, physical or psychological, is a clue to the working of the unconscious which should be followed up at the right time. But, if we feel this deadly kind of guilt, it simply means that we cannot accept our human condition, that we have given way to *hubris* and are saying unconsciously, "I ought to be like God, free of all weakness," forgetting what happened to God himself on the cross. The clues are to be worked upon, but the symptom itself is something to be wholly and freely accepted without egotistic guilt or any *demand* to be freed from it.

Hope for release is another thing, both natural and right, as also are the exterior efforts to come out of the sickness or mood. We are not excused from ordinary common sense by the fact that we accept the suffering and demand no release. In fact the two attitudes are one, and real acceptance will lead us to seek the appropriate help, whether medical skill in illness, the support of friends in grief, rest in exhaustion, work either physical or psychological in depression. Thus, we begin to build the "undercarriage" of suffering upon which the superstructure of our lives may securely rest and under which the wheels may move freely over the earth. The four-wheeled chariot is an ancient symbol of the Incarnation, and the thought of suffering as the undercarriage fits perfectly into this image. Suffering is that which carries the weight of the vehicle, distributing it over the fourfold wheels so that the driver may stand in safety and move toward his chosen goal.

However great our efforts may be to achieve this conscious attitude to suffering we cannot succeed without an awareness that, in spite of apparent senselessness, there is always an implicit universal meaning even in the carrying of small miseries. Every time a person exchanges neurotic depression for real suffering he or she is sharing to some small degree in the carrying of the suffering of mankind, in bearing a tiny part of the darkness of the world. Such a one is released from his small personal concern into a sense of *meaning*. One may not be consciously thinking in these terms, but the transition can immediately be recognized by the disappearance of the frustrated pointlessness of mood and depression. It is as though we become aware of a new dimension. Meaning has entered the experience.

We may be emotionally moved and filled with horror and pity when we hear of the tragedies of human lives at a distance, but the emotions lift no burden, they carry nothing. In contrast, the smallest consent to the fierce, sharp pain of objective suffering in the most trivial-seeming matter may have an influence, as the Chinese sage puts it, "at a distance of a thousand miles." We may be entirely certain that some burden somewhere is lightened by our effort. Close at hand the effects are often immediately visible. Those around us may know nothing of what is happening but a weight is lifted from the atmosphere, or someone we love is set free to be himself, and the sufferer acquires a new clarity of vision and sensitivity to another's need. Nothing is as blinding as neurotic self-pity. We walk around in a fog.

There is a familiar example of the difference between objective suffering and subjective emotional reaction in its effect on others, which many people have experienced at some time in their lives if they have been seriously ill. A nurse, or anyone else who is close to another's pain, physical or psychic, if she reacts with intense personal emotion to the patient's misery, will either repress what she cannot bear and become hard and unfeeling or else will increase the sick one's burden through her unconscious identification. A true nurse, by contrast, is always deeply concerned; she is compassionate (which means objectively "suffering with") but not invaded by emotional reactions. She is herself changed by the experience through the love that lives beyond emotion. The patient can literally be saved by this kind of "carrying" by another, but can be swamped and pushed deeper into misery by the unconscious reactions of those around him or her, however well they may be disguised. The difference is subtle but absolutely distinct when experienced.

Just as there is no cure for an inferior kind of love except a greater and more conscious love, so there is no cure for inferior suffering except a greater kind of suffering. It is possible by intense conscious attention to pass through this door into the fiercer suffering which is linked to the whole, and then a strange thing may happen. We have lifted the weight and, instead of being crushed by it, we find it extraordinarily light—"My yoke is easy, my burden is light"(Matt. 11:30). The pain remains but it is more like the piercing of a sword than a weight. "A sword shall pierce through thy own soul also that the thoughts of many hearts may be revealed"(Luke 2:35). These are the prophetic words of the wise old man Simeon, spoken to Mary when she took her newborn child to the temple. We have shed blood, the sacrificial blood, and so we can experience joy, not just pleasant feelings and escape.

There is in man a fear of joy as keen as the fear of suffering pain, because true joy precludes the pleasant feeling of self-importance just as suffering precludes all the comforts of self-pity. No man can know the one without the other. It is important here to discriminate between the spurious joy of the martyr complex and the joy which is on the other side of the cross. Christ was not a martyr, going singing to his death. If we catch ourselves feeling noble on account of our sufferings we may be perfectly sure that we are simply at the old trick of climbing out of depression into pleasant feeling—all the more dangerous because it is camouflaged as noble.

Real suffering belongs to innocence, not guilt. As long as we feel misery because we are full of remorse and guilt or shame over our weakness, all we experience is a loss of vital energy and no transformation takes place. But the minute we accept objectively the guilt and shame, the *innocent* part of us begins to suffer, the weight becomes a sword. We bleed, and the energy flows back into us on a deeper and more conscious level. This is real repentance as opposed to ego-centered shame, for it involves the recognition of the true guilt which lies always in our evasions of objective awareness.

For Christians, it is easy to give lip service to the "innocent victim," to Christ carrying in innocence the sin and suffering of the world. But rarely do we even think of the essential practical application of this truth in the smallest of our pains. Only when the *innocent* part of us begins to suffer is there life and creation within and around us; but for the most part we prefer to remain caught in the vicious and totally unproductive circle of remorse and superficial complacency, followed by a repetition of the sin, more remorse, and so on. In the Book of Job, God's condemnation falls on the complacent rationality of the false comforters who assure Job that he could not possibly be suffering unless he were morally guilty. To Job, suffering but innocent, God's answer is simply to reveal himself in his infinite power and glory, beyond rational explanation.

In these days when the media bring to us daily the sight and sound of the appalling sufferings of the innocent, we all have great need of reminders of the only way in which we can contribute to the healing of the terrible split between curse and blessing in our time.

The poets and great story-tellers of all ages come to our aid. When one man takes up the responsibility for his blindness without any false guilt, even in the smallest things, the self-pity and the projections of blame onto others or onto God drops away, and the blessing beyond the opposites is strengthened in our environment. It seems infinitesimal, but in Jung's words it may be the "makeweight that tips the scales." Thus we suffer the sword of objectivity, refusing nothing, so that the healing may reach "the hearts of many" without our conscious intention. It happens not through our willed efforts to improve the world, fine and right though these may be on another level, but to the degree to which the curse and the blessing have been experienced consciously as one in the psyche of the individual. It is an experience which, as C.G. Jung wrote in *Mysterium Conjunctionis,* reaches "the individual in stillness—the individual who constitutes the meaning of the world."

We began by defining a word. We end with another—the word "passion." Derived from the Latin *passio,* meaning suffering, it is used to define the suffering of Christ. Commonly the word applies to any emotion which goes beyond the bounds of reason, consuming and possessing a man so that he is in a state of "enthusiasm," which, in its original meaning, is the state of being filled with the god, whether the god of anger, of love, or of hate.

When suffering breaks through the small personal context and exposes a man to the pain and darkness of life itself, the way is opened to that ultimate state of passion beyond all the passions of desire. There, being completely empty, as Christ was empty when he cried, "My God, my God, why hast Thou forsaken me," he may finally come to be filled with the wholeness of God himself.

12

The Lord's Prayer

M any people have interpreted the Our Father in the language of each age—in our own century notably Charles Williams and Simone Weil, but both are of the generation ending with the Second World War—and we may again perhaps approach it and attempt to see some of its unchanging meanings in the language of our own day. The prayer is a miracle of brevity, for it deals in far less than one hundred words with what we may call the four great "matters" of human life: the relationship between creator and created, between spirit and nature; the matter of food; the nature of forgiveness; and our attitudes to temptation and evil.

"Our Father which art in Heaven." In the old English form of the King James version, the "which" can be a hint of the essential impersonality of the Father added to his aspect as Person. The "who" can subtly increase the temptation to reduce the Creator from Person to a personality, to the benevolent or frightening all-powerful father figure who will rescue us from our troubles or before whom we cringe in guilt. We may think we have long outgrown such childish ideas, but in fact this attitude to the Creator is so bred into our unconscious that we are very frequently caught in such an attitude—every time, for instance, we are gripped by false guilts or expect to be spoon-fed, or demand our so-called "rights." The prayer starts with a categorical warning against all such anthropomorphising of God. "Our Father *which art in Heaven.*" That which created us and all life exists in totality in Heaven—far beyond the reach of our earthly consciousness. At the time of Christ the image invoked by the word *Father* was surely different from that which possesses us today—a far simpler thing, meaning "he who gives us life." For us it has become a dangerous word to use in our speaking of God and the emphasis in this first clause must lie heavily on the second half—"which art in heaven"—with the implication, as Simone Weil says, that God is not and must never be addressed as our father upon earth. "If we think to have a Father here on earth, it is not he—it is a false god."

As Jung has so often pointed out, we know, and can know with the human reason, absolutely nothing about the objective nature of the utterly transcendent creator in heaven, and it is dangerous folly to imagine that we can. "Hallowed be Thy Name." His name is holy, whole, and any of the partial concepts of him by which we think to name him are nothing but the projections of our own infantile desires and fears. For this reason it was forbidden to the Jews to speak the name of God—"Hear, O Israel, the Lord Our God is One" (Deut. 6:4). The Jewish people had discovered this tremendous truth, and because of it God could no longer be named. The gods of the pagan world are another matter—the more precisely they are named the better, for they are the symbolic images of man's infinitely varied approach to the divine, and their danger lay in the fact that they were for most an end in themselves, thus inducing a blindness to the One. But the realization of the One God brought its own danger—the unconscious of man, deprived of the symbolic gods, became identified with these partial systems and projected them onto the One himself, pulling him down to the level of some small, half-human deity. Only in the consciousness of the individuated man or woman can these projections, these confusions of end and means, be resolved. It is by this we sense that the Creator is incomprehensible to the human reason—Person as well as not person—because only a truly intuitive individual can experience his reality and say, as Jung did, "I do not believe; I know."

That, however, which we cannot know of the Father in his totality in Heaven we can and must experience in terms of earth. "Thy kingdom come, Thy will be done in earth as it is in Heaven." Here again, the old form of words, "in earth," is so much more powerful than the modern "on earth." The seed of the creative must descend into the earth, not on top of the earth, and be hidden in her womb, in order that the kingdom, the rule of the One, may be born, the Will be done, and the awareness of Tao, of the dance of creation, may awaken in man. The opening of the prayer asserts that at the root of all is the Father in Heaven, the Creator, the total holiness, and at all times we must affirm this transcendence, but it is wholly meaningless if we stand gazing upwards, trying to lift our feet off the earth and identifying with a nebulous goodness dwelling ever in the light with no darkness to cloud it. We do this to some degree whenever we refuse to accept any *fact*. Only in the darkness of the earth can the Kingdom be real to us.

"All creation is feminine to God," it has been said. For us, this means to be wholly receptive to the seed of the creative in every smallest and most insignificant movement of the dance here in our earth nature, be it "good" or "bad," light or dark. The moment we reject a fact of any kind, inner or outer, the creative remains remote, unmanifest, a mere concept, far beyond us in Heaven, and we are nothing but split-off, empty imitations of man. Whenever we accept a fact, accept with a will to rejoice, not just resigning ourselves to it, with all its causes in the past and all its potentialities in the future, then the seed is sown, the individual moves a tiny step toward consciousness, and so his will is done in earth and we have perhaps a glimpse of the unity "as it is in Heaven," of eternity and time as one thing.

"Give us this day our daily bread." This is not at all the same thing as "see that we have bread to eat today." Either "give us bread today" or "give us our daily bread" would convey this meaning, but the words "*this day* our daily bread" speak of something much more subtle. We may infer that the petition is not for bread to be produced, for it is there all the time—the daily bread, the food of life, everything that we need to nourish us. The Israelites had no need each day to petition the Lord for the manna. They knew it would be there, morning by morning, lying thick on the ground. To have persistently reminded God of his promise would have been a failure in courtesy if nothing else. No, the petition is surely a cry that we may be aware enough to *eat* this daily offered bread *today,* in this present moment—that we may not, like many of the Israelites, imagine that we can either pick it up and hoard it for tomorrow, or that we can ignore it today and eat twice as much the next day. (I am too busy today, I am feeling too bad to attend to the inner voice—a dream, an image. There is no time to be still, to go to where the manna lies waiting.)

Hence, the insistence in all religions, all systems of meditation, on all the ways to consciousness, from primitive sun worship to Jung's way of individuation, on *daily* attention. If a day is missed, there is a sliding back into the fog, however imperceptible. How essential, then, is this cry: "give us the strength and courage to eat *this day* the food that every smallest experience of our daily lives offers us if we will consciously eat it, swallow it, digest it as it is—not as we wish it could be, lusting after the flesh pots, as did the Israelites." We may feel on most days unsatisfied, undernourished, but every smallest effort to *attend* is the eating of the tasteless, colorless manna, and an imperceptible change takes place out of sight in our depths.

There are two translations of the next clause. "Forgive us our trespasses as we forgive them that trespass against us" and "Forgive us our debts as we forgive our debtors." They express different aspects of the same thing. To trespass is to pass over our own boundaries and intrude on the territory of others—to invade the sphere of the gods, to meddle in the affairs, manipulate the psyche of another, to fail in respect for the boundary between the human and the animal, to treat even inanimate things with possessiveness or contempt—all this is trespass. It goes on constantly in all of us and no conscious determination to avoid it is by itself of any help at all. In fact every unconscious part of us is inevitably living outside our boundaries, wandering loose, an intruder, whether in Heaven, Hell, or our neighbor's garden.

Every time we *demand* changes in ourselves, in people, in facts, forgetful of the Fool whose dance makes a harmony of all, then we trespass and clumsily stamp out the possibility of real change and growth. The person who seems to the superficial observer to be most aloof, uninterested in the affairs of others, may even be a worse offender than the more obvious trespasser, through unconscious fantasies that proliferate out of sight, so that no one is real to him at all as a separate individual to whom he is related, and his unconscious is lived in projection even "to a distance of a thousand miles," as the Chinese say. The isolation of his outer life is compensated for by an unbridled trespassing within. Jung has said that a man can only discover himself when he is deeply and unconditionally related to some, and generally related to a great many, individuals with whom he has a chance to compare and from whom he is able to discriminate himself. "Related to," not "mixed with," and relationship is impossible when there is trespassing. One very common example of the difficulty of this is the way we confuse real concern and kindness to another with "benevolent" interference, which is an invasion or trespass. It is exceedingly difficult to be a man or a woman—related to (and therefore distinct from) our own inner figures, to the gods, to other men and women, to animals and things, and we begin to grow to this stature in the proportion that we are forgiven our trespasses.

"Forgive us our trespasses *as we forgive.*" There is only one way to the forgiveness that frees us from crippling guilt and it lies in the willingness to "forgive them that trespass," that is, to forgive not only the trespassing that the projections of others inflict upon us, but the trespassing of our own inner figures, such as anima and animus, who thrust themselves into our outer lives, leaving their proper sphere, invading our will, distorting our feeling and our actions. No one can forgive another until he can discriminate himself from that other. Still less can he forgive an inner figure while identified with him. And it is here that the hard road of forgiveness begins—in the discrimination of ourselves from the powers of the unconscious that possess us and so, from within our own boundaries, forgive. And since we can hardly forgive "complexes," we must see them as personified images of the unconscious. Only then does it become possible for us as separate and distinct individuals to forgive each other, and in the exact proportion to which we are able wholly to forgive do we experience the extraordinary freedom and blessedness of knowing ourselves forgiven and set free to love.

It is a common delusion that forgiveness is a comfortable forgetfulness of injury, following easily on an apology or on the recognition of a fault. But this is a far cry from true forgiveness, and it usually springs from a kind of self-satisfied superiority. Forgiveness is a state of mind and heart, a condition of gratitude, one might say, to *all* the manifestations of life, inner and outer, no matter how negatively they may affect us. It is absolutley unconditional or it is nothing. As long as we can discover in ourselves the smallest rejection of a person, a thing, or a fact, then we do not forgive. This is the very opposite of condoning with soft words the evil thing in another or in ourselves. It involves the most clear-sighted discrimination between dark and light—

an infinitely hard and constantly renewed refusal to accept the half-truths with which we comfortably cover up our trespassing and that of others, together with a total willingness to accept the person or the fact. Every time we do this we are ourselves forgiven and some part of our trespassing is redeemed and made whole.

"Forgive us our debts as we forgive our debtors." The word *debt* opens up the whole matter of *karma,* as it is called in Hindu philosophy. Every single act or thought or feeling of the ego opposed to the Self must be paid for before a man can be freed from "the wheel of existence." Unless the opposites are transcended, their unity known in full consciousness, then they continually constellate and compensate each other, and the so-called "good" we do out of our ego-consciousness produces an equal amount of "bad" in the unconscious. Nothing is really changed, there is no true *metanoia,* whatever the appearances. There is only one way, then, whereby our debts may be forgiven, our karma remitted. We are freed from this inevitable law of compensation to the exact degree in which we can achieve forgiveness of that which we conceive to be owed to us. Simone Weil has written most powerfully of this. She says:

> At the moment of saying these words we must have already remitted everything that is owing to us. This not only includes reparation for any wrongs we think we have suffered, but also gratitude for the good we think we have done, and it applies in a quite general way to all we expect from people and things, to all we consider as our due and without which we should feel ourselves to have been frustrated. All these are the rights that we think the past has given us over the future.[1]

"Lead us not into temptation, but deliver us from evil." "How could that which is Love," it may be asked, "lead anyone into temptation?" "Surely it is the devil who does that." Yes, it is that dark side of God, which man refuses so that it needs to become the Devil to him—Lucifer, the fallen son of God, who brings consciousness to us all as he did in the desert to Christ himself, making him aware of the extreme dangers involved in the coming of the Son of God to earth. Jesus' temptations were all concerned with the deliberate misuse of consciousness, of the awareness of the Self. This is the evil from which we indeed must cry out to be delivered. Weaknesses, unconscious projections, trespasses, all these must be faced and struggled with, but they are not evil. Evil is the use of the power, the manna, set free by increasing consciousness, for the purposes of the ego, no matter how seemingly positive and "good for others" these purposes may be, and it is the temptation to which every breakthrough exposes us. The ego, feeling in itself a new sense of power, may start to turn stones to bread to evade the starkness of the desert, calling things by false names to appease its own hunger or that of others. Ot it may feel so inflated as to set itself up as an embodiment of truth (whether to the world or to only one other makes little difference), throwing itself down from the temple, as it were, to demonstrate how free it is from the ordinary laws; or it may even more deliberately delude itself that personal power and domination is for the good of its environment, and so fall down and worship the devil himself, who is the identification of God with the ego's will to power.

"He was led of the Spirit into the wilderness to be tempted of the devil" (Matt. 4:1). We may cry in our weakness that the way not lead us into these temptations, but we know in our hearts that the Spirit will most surely lead us into the wilderness and that, once there, the tempter will come. But in being led into the wilderness, we are also led to the great opportunity, the experience wherein, through the fullest confrontation with the devil of which we are capable, we are enabled to say "no" to the arrogance of the ego playing God, or its opposite which is despair. Then we may indeed be freed, in the words of the Athanasian Creed, from "confusion of substance" and glimpse at last the "unity of person"; but this can only be when we are humble enough to know that only by the grace of God are we delivered from this final evil (symbolized in J.R.R. Tolkien's *Lord of the Rings* by the taking and wearing of the "ring of power" for any purpose whatsoever) and never by our own effort alone. The light of consciousness must be sought with every fiber of our being, but can never be surely found until, at the last, it is known as "given."

Part Three

IMAGES

13

Two Tales

Salmon-Fisher Boy

He was known to the few who lived on the mountain as Salmon-Fisher Boy. He had no other name. He lived with the old grandmother in the woods and wandered, free and happy, through the days, returning in the evening to the old woman's fireside to eat freshly baked bread with the rich soup from her big round pot hanging over the flames. On most days he could be seen lying flat on his stomach on the bank of the small river that ran through the woods, at a place in a small, hidden valley where the rocks contained a deep, clear pool of the flowing river water. He would lie gazing into the pool, very still, and often he would gently plunge his arm down through the water reaching out to the dark shape of the old fish that lay at the base of the rock. Little fishes flicked past his arm, unafraid and indifferent, but he paid no heed to them. The great salmon that lived in the pool, gliding, sliding through the clear water, dark with a glint of silver where the sun struck down at midday—this was his concern.

Sometimes when the boy was still enough, quiet enough, Old Fish, Wise Fish, would, with a slight powerful movement of his fins, rise swiftly through the water and briefly touch the boy's fingers with his head before turning in a perfection of grace to pour his great length down again to the bottom, where he lay again a dark shadow beside the dark rock, swaying with the gentle movement of the water. When this happened, Salmon-Fisher Boy knew perfect content. Old Fish, Wise Fish, had spoken to him and he had heard, though the speech had no words; and as he ran happily back through the wood he felt, could he have spoken it, that Old Fish, Wise Fish, went with him in the clear air, and that yet together they were gliding, sliding through the dark water of the pool, and that nothing could break the joy of this secret.

One such day in the autumn of the year the boy had been lying still and happy for a long time beside the pool. It was time to go when something compelled him to strip off his shirt and plunge both his arms to the shoulders down into the water. Then suddenly to his astonishment and joy he saw the great fish rising. He came higher than ever before to the level of the boy's elbows, and then swam slowly in a figure of eight between and around his arms. The boy did not move as the fish swam free into the center of the pool and then leaped out of the water in a great arc of silver, touched with gold by the setting sun, and plunged down again to disappear completely under the rock. Now he rose and in a daze of wonder and happiness turned homewards. Soon he was running with eager thoughts of supper and the long evening ahead with the old grandmother, when they would sit together by the fire and she would tell him stories of the birds and beasts and fishes and, most fascinating of all, of the ways of the salmon and of their journey to and from the great sea. He had never spoken of Old Fish, Wise Fish, but somehow he was sure that she knew him too. He was one of those few who had stayed long in the sea, and, bringing its stored wisdom with him, had now come up the river to the pool and would not return.

This evening, as the boy came to the open door of the cottage, he stood still and felt the brush of fear. The sound of a man's voice came to him from inside, and instinctively, though he heard no words, he knew that the man was talking about him. Slowly the boy moved forward through the doorway. "Here you are, boy!" said the voice. It was a kind voice yet somehow stern and cold in the boy's ears. "I have come to take you away now to school, for you are no longer a child, and it is time for you to learn many things and to see the great world and meet the people in it, so that you may grow to be a man of learning and be able to do some worthy work and earn your bread."

Slowly the boy raised his head and looked the man in the eyes. "Yes," he whispered. It was as though he had always known that someday this must come. "Good boy," said the man. "Now what is your name?'' ''My name is S-s-almon-Fisher B-b-,'' he stuttered. He had never spoken this name, the only name he knew, before, and it now sounded all wrong, whereas unspoken, it had seemed to fit him like a glove. But the man interrupted, ''Oh yes, 'Sam Fisher,' a good name. Well, Sam, be ready in the morning. I will come for you early.'' He bowed to old grandmother and was gone. Stunned, the boy turned to the old woman. Her usually merry twinkling eyes were sad, but she came to him and took his hands in hers. ''It has to be,'' she said, ''but do not ever forget, dear boy, whatever may come to you, your true unalterable name. You are the Salmon-Fisher Boy. Remember this in your heart as I will remember it in mine, and you will not lose Old Fish, Wise Fish, who, I know as I look at you, has laid upon you this day the sign of the wisdom of the Fish. Now go to bed and sleep and tomorrow go to meet the new without fear!''

The journey to the south was long, and the boy's spirits rose as he eagerly absorbed the sights and sounds that were so new to him. His companion was gentle and told him many stories of the countryside and of the cities through which the train passed. Arrived at the school, the boy suffered much at first from homesickness and the strange confined life, but his longing to learn was strong and some of his classes were good, which his growing mind happily absorbed. So the time passed and his memories of the old life began to fade. Yet he remained always, in some way that he did not understand, an alien among his fellows. The other children liked him. He joined in their games and their interests, but from everything in the school life a part of him remained aloof. Perhaps the others felt this, for he was never teased or bullied—he was respected and perhaps unconsciously a little feared, for children shun the strange and the different. As he grew older this alien feeling began to grow stronger. The boy hated and rejected this thing in himself and tried to throw himself into the life more wholeheartedly, but the effort merely increased his trouble. He found himself losing interest in both work and play. Worst of all, the teachers whom he most respected, alarmed at his listlessness, began to press him, to reproach him, to urge him to greater effort, holding out to him pictures of the future, of worldly and intellectual success which, they said, he had the ability to achieve. He was bewildered, not understanding why he could not respond, and sank into a sullen hopelessness.

One day he lay out on the playing fields, alone, lethargic and without hope. Suddenly he heard a woman's voice. He looked up and saw a stranger on whose face was a deep concern. "What is the matter with you?" she asked. "Do you need a holiday? I'll ask if you may come away for awhile and stay with me." Then he heard another voice answer. It was an older boy whom he knew only slightly, but who, alone of all the people at the school, had often looked at him as though he understood. This boy spoke to the woman and said, "A holiday would do him no good at all. He is being badgered here to become something which will kill him." "What does he really want to do?" she asked. "He wants to fish for salmon," replied the tall boy, "though he has almost forgotten it himself." The woman bent down and took the boy's hands pulling him to his feet. "Come with me," she said, "we will go to the authorities and you shall leave this place, and I will take you to those who will teach you to be a fisherman."

And so it came about that the boy travelled north once more. The woman took him to a tiny village where the mountains rose on three sides, and on the fourth side was the sea. Only one small road, too steep for motor traffic, led down to this village and all their supplies came to the little bay by boat. The woman and boy came in the evening to a stone-built cottage, where lived a tall, strong fisherman with graying hair and his quiet wife. Their children were all grown up and had left the village, and the woman knew they would take the boy in as though he were their own son. Fish fresh from the sea was frying in the pan as they walked through the door, the peat fire glowed on the hearth; the fisherman's wife smiled a true welcome. The boy's lethargy dropped from him in that moment, never to return. Tomorrow he would go out and begin to learn the ways of boats, the lore of the nets and the fishing lines, of winds and tides. He turned, radiant, to thank the woman who had brought him, but she was gone.

So began his new life. He was eager, fearless, happy, intelligent, and so he learned fast and his skill was a delight to his foster parents. Years passed and he was now a tall, strong young fisherman whose fame began to spread up and down that coast of fishermen. For added to his skill he had, it was said, the most extraordinary luck. Whenever he was out with a trawler, the nets were always full; if he went out alone with a line he came home with a catch large enough to feed almost the whole of his tiny village. He moved now from his beloved foster home into a small cottage of his own nearby and all expected him to seek a wife and settle down to family life. Everywhere he had friends, both men and women, but always there remained that strange core of aloofness and none could say they shared his inmost thoughts. He did not marry; not that he was cold—far from it— and he himself did not know why he felt it impossible. It was as though the sea itself were his beloved, and coming back from a night of encounter with wind and storm, or the quiet of calm, dark water under the moon he was fulfilled. He became known affectionately as Fisher Sam, instead of Sam Fisher, and few men begrudged his luck.

There was one silent, almost morose old man with whom he constantly sailed. They exchanged no thoughts, but with him Fisher Sam felt a closeness and an understanding that no one else shared. One day as they sat mending their nets the old man said, "You have caught every kind of sea fish, Sam, but you have never been up the river with a rod to fish for salmon. Let's take a holiday and go inland." Sam felt his heart leap with excitement, but also a strange reluctance. He was silent for several minutes, then answered, "Yes, it is time I went up the river. There is grey in my hair already."

So they sailed up the coast to the mouth of the river, moored their boat, and started on foot up into the mountains. They camped overnight beside the river and in the early dawn went out to cast their lines. Fisher Sam watched the old man, who was an expert angler, as he made the first cast. Almost at once a salmon bit and as the old man landed it, Sam, that fisherman of long experience, had a strange and violent reaction. His whole being revolted at the sight of the dying fish—faint memories stirred in his heart—and he turned and plunged in among the trees bewildered and ashamed at the violence of his feeling. He wandered restlessly for hours and then lay down under a tree and fell immediately into a deep sleep. He dreamed, and in his dream he saw himself lying beside a clear, deep pool of the river and staring down into the water where a great salmon lay near the bottom. The fish was slowly rising toward him and as his head broke the surface, he spoke.

"I am Old Fish, Wise Fish," he said. "You have forgotten me in your head but never in your heart and soul. Years ago I, or my grandfather, no matter, set upon you the sign of the fish, and one day when you are old, you will come back to this pool. But you still have work to do. Do not hesitate to cast your line and catch the salmon. Men need fish to eat, need it desperately. They are surfeited with the red meat of animals. Food from the rivers, food from the sea, this is the nourishment their souls crave. And most of all, they need salmon, for we are kings among fishes. Do you not know that what men call your 'luck' is no such thing? You carry the 'sign of the fish' and all our kind will offer themselves to your net or your line, for you fish for love not for greed. You were the Salmon-Fisher Boy."

Sam woke and lay very still. His lifelong feeling that a part of himself was shut away had disappeared. All things fell into place with an intensity of meaning that flooded his whole being. He rose and saw that it was evening. Beside the river the old man had returned to fish again and Sam now joined him quietly and spoke. "We will go home now," he said. "I am going to move from the sea and live up here beside the river to catch salmon for the villages." The old man asked no questions, simply nodded in understanding. Sam knew now that he, too, had been marked with the sign of the fish.

And so for many more years Sam lived beside the river and people far and wide ate of the salmon he caught. There came a day in his old age when he knew it was time to leave—to fish no more. He packed his few necessities in a bundle, walked out of his house, leaving behind his beloved rods, and set off up river. For three days he climbed higher into the mountains, led by an instinct that he trusted but could not explain. On the third day he stood on a flat rock and looked down on the pool of his dream—and not only of his dream, he now knew. Memory flooded back, the little boy, Salmon-Fisher Boy, lying there on the rock with his arms in the water and Old Fish, Wise Fish, swimming around them in the figure of eight. He saw, too, his grandmother in her cottage, and turning, he strode unerringly along the path through the forest to its door and stopped. A very thin but clear, calm voice called to him. "Come in, Salmon-Fisher Boy. I have been waiting for you." He entered and there lay old grandmother on her bed, very old now, frail, almost transparent, but with the same twinkle in her eyes and a peace surrounding her that soothed all unrest. "Now I can go, dear boy," she said. "This is your home and here you will live, not fishing anymore, but passing onto those few who will come to you the wisdom of the fish."

He knelt beside her and took her hand as she closed her eyes. So they stayed as the sun sank slowly, and when the fisherman rose to light the lamp, he saw that she had quietly died. He covered her gently and stood in the doorway, his eyes on the crescent moon in the fading glow of the sunset. An end and a beginning. He had come home.

The Hunter and the Hunted

The hunter stood still—still without the tiniest movement, his bow in hand, gazing into the mist ahead of him. "Gazelle," he thought, and his heart lifted. He was upwind, the herd was moving slowly toward him as it grazed, and the mist would soon be gone under the morning sun. The hunter was not young. His hair was grizzled and his face lined with the mark of years, but his body remained strong and supple and his eyes keen. Few other hunters of the tribe could match his skill. Now, as he stood like a stone and waited, he saw that one of the herd was ahead of the others, that he grazed alone, and the hunter caught his breath. "A chief among gazelle," he murmured as the mist lifted and he saw the size and beauty and grace of the noble animal, the long tapering horns, the slender neck, the graceful strength of the legs, and the body built for speed. Almost he wished to shoot an arrow harmlessly into the air for the utter delight it always gave him to see gazelle in motion, flying as it were over the rolling plain. But he knew that he must take home food.

He concentrated now on his task as hunter—judging the distance, marking with his eye the spot over the heart that he would hope to hit so that the animal might die quickly and with little pain. Slowly, very slowly, he had begun to move his hand up to take an arrow from his quiver when a sound from behind him turned him rigid. Only his perfect discipline kept him from a quick turn, which would have sent the gazelle in a few swift bounds to safety—his discipline and also his recognition of the sound. He had heard it before, that sound of a twanging bowstring like no other bowstring—not often, but on all the great days of his hunting life, and always it carried with it a strange feeling, compounded of fear and excitement, that behind him was one who hunted *him* as he hunted his game. When young he had turned quickly and angrily as the sound reached him, ready to meet and fight this enemy who pursued him. But always behind him was emptiness and silence. He remembered now the first time it had happened. When hunting with his father as a boy, he had made his first kill and his heart was high with pride. As they moved toward the dead quarry, he had heard the twanging bow and had jumped round in fear, feeling for the first time the terror of the hunted beating down the pride of the hunter. His father had questioned him. "What ails you, boy?" And stumblingly he had told of his strange feeling and of the sound he had heard. His father had looked long and deeply into his eyes, saying no word. At last he spoke. "My son," he said, "Tell no one of this thing. If it should come again, ask no questions either of others or of yourself—and the day may dawn when you will have no need to ask." He had obeyed, but, from that time on, the exhilaration of the hunt, and the joyful pride of the kill had carried with them an undercurrent of sadness and pain, for he knew within himself the panic fear of the hunted as the bowstring twanged and the arrow flew to its mark.

He had schooled himself through the years not even to turn his head when he heard the bow of the Great Hunter (as he had named the unseen), but the moment of terror could not be schooled and he had learned to accept it together with the hidden pain it left behind in his heart.

This time, he thought, it seemed nearer than ever before—he had even imagined for an instant a sharp pain in his back—but his eyes never left his quarry, and his hand, checked for that brief moment, moved on toward the quiver. Now as his fingers touched an arrow his stillness vanished and in one incredibly swift movement he had strung it, bent his bow, and shot. The beautiful creature, realizing his peril too late, fell as he gathered himself for flight, the arrow striking deep into his side but not to the heart. The hunter ran now, drawing out his knife to end quickly the pain of the gazelle, but as he reached the dying animal he stumbled and fell and the knife flew from his hand. He raised himself to his knees and found that he was gazing straight into the eye of his kill, the soft brown antelope eyes, the unfathomably mysterious eyes of the animal. Then, without warning, he felt a pair of very strong, yet gentle, hands covering his eyes and bearing him backward and sideways until he lay with his head on the body of the gazelle. Wondering at himself, the hunter did not resist. He lay still and waited, for he knew with absolute certainty that he, the hunter and the hunted, had finally been brought to bay by that other unknown and he waited for death quietly, as his gazelle also waited with the life blood pouring from its side. The hands were withdrawn from his eyes and, as he had looked from above into the eyes of the hunted, he looked now from below into the eyes of the hunter, and he smiled as he knew and recognized the unknown who bent over him, holding his own fallen knife poised above his heart. "Strike now," he said and closed his eyes. A searing pain shot through him as the knife cut the flesh between his breast bones and a mist came down and he lay as though dead.

The afternoon sun was slanting toward the West as he opened his eyes in wonder that he lived. He looked down at his breast—a deep cut was there—the knife had drawn a perfect circular furrow and the blood had flowed, and falling had mingled with the blood of the gazelle, now dead. The wound was not deep—already the bleeding had stopped, but the circle of the scar would remain to the end of his days. His knife lay beside him and he picked it up to begin the skinning of his kill. Then he stayed his hand, his heart beating fast. The gazelle lay with its head thrown back, its white throat and chest exposed, and in the center of that whiteness was a clear circle of dark hair. "The King Gazelle! He is the King!"

The hunter sheathed his knife. He knew now the meaning—the meaning of the unknown hunter, of his lying under the knife, of the circle on his own breast. He had killed the King gazelle and he would hunt no more. For once, once in a generation perhaps, a hunter would bring home the King gazelle—bring him intact, unskinned, to the elders, and then that hunter must give up his beloved bow, his knife, his home and his wife, and go to live in the house of the 'Hunter and the Hunted" as it was called (he had never understood before the true meaning of the house for no one ever spoke of it). He would join the wise old ones of the tribe, who killed no more but who tended the dark and the light, the fire and the water, the dance and the dreams of them all. He lifted the gazelle and carried it over his shoulders like a yoke as he walked steadily back to the tents away to the East.

A woman stood alone beside the stream to the West of the encampment. Small, grey-haired but erect, she was very still, waiting, watching for her man as the shadows lengthened. He came at last, weary and sweating, bent almost double by the weight of the animal. Pausing by the stepping stones across the stream, he put down his burden to rest and his eyes lit up to see her cross swiftly to meet him. They did not speak but the hunter pointed silently to the dark circle on the chest of the dead gazelle. She gave it a brief quiet glance. "I knew," she said, "Indeed I have known the day would come, for your mother told me before I came to your tent that you were a hunted one." She bent down to the clear running water and filled an earthenware bowl she carried. "Drink," she said. He took it in both hands and drank deeply, then bathed his face and hands and washed the blood from the circle on his breast. But now his face was drawn with suffering and he turned again to her with tears in his eyes, reaching for her hands. "My husband and my love," she said, "the knife cuts deep in both our hearts, but the parting is clean and whole and holds no bitterness, as when death rends a pattern half complete. Go now and fear not for me. Our stream divides, but all water flows forever to the sea. The news of your coming has spread and all are gathered at the place of council to greet you, and my joy in you is great." Her voice trembled slightly on the words. He kissed her gravely on the brow and lifting his kill again onto his shoulders, he passed over the stream and out of her human life.

She sat long beside the stream as the twilight darkened and the sun sank behind the hill—and the sound of the water entered into her and brought peace. Then she rose and walked slowly back toward her tent. All the others, men, women, and children would be at the great ceremony, watching the skinning of the King gazelle, the clothing of her man in its royal skin. And then they would feast and dance, dance all through the night the greatest and rarest of the dances—the dance of the hunter and the hunted. But she must sit alone in her tent tonight. Her heart failed her for a moment as she braced herself to face the emptiness of that long-shared place, where they had lain in the joy of their youth, where she had borne her sons and daughters, where she and he had loved and laughed together in the perfect companionship of later years. She reached the threshold and paused, hearing a rustle. Then merry laughter greeted her as out of the dark tent rushed two small vigorous figures, one clutching at each of her hands. "Grandmother," they said, jumping up and down. "Grandmother, they have all gone to some big meeting and we hate crowds, so we ran away here to you. Tell us a story, Grandmother dear, tell us a story—please, please do!"

The woman smiled and hugged them both—the boy and the girl, her youngest twin six-year-old grandchildren. "Very well," she said, "but first we must build a campfire. Come, little ones, gather sticks and I will kindle it." The children obeyed eagerly and soon the flames were leaping, the three were squatting round the fire, and the children gazed raptly and expectantly at the old woman. "Once upon a time," she began, "once upon a time. . . ." And at those timeless words all gaps were closed. Together the old and the young, the wise and the innocent, entered the gate and passed into that country where yesterday and today and tomorrow meet. "Once upon a time there was a hunter whose name was 'Swift Gazelle' . . . ."

Notes

Introduction

1. C. G. Jung, *Letters of C. G. Jung,* vol. 2 of *The Collected Works,* The Bollingen Series (Princeton: Princeton University Press, 1975), p. 364.
2. M. R. James, *The Apocryphal New Testament* (Oxford; Clarendon, 1953), p. 33.
3. Jung, *Letters,* p. 364.
4. C. G. Jung, *Psychology and Religion,* vol. 11 of *The Collected Works,* The Bollingen Series (Princeton University Press, 1958), p. 347.

Chapter 3 / The Religious Vows of Poverty, Chastity, and Obedience

1. Max Plowman, *An Introduction to the Study of Blake* (New York: Barnes and Noble, 1967), pp. 128–29.
2. Charles Williams, *He Came Down from Heaven* (London: Faber and Faber, 1950), p. 25.
3. Plowman, pp. 79–81.
4. Quoted by Plowman, p. 24.

Chapter 4 / The Mystery Within

1. C. G. Jung, *Alchemical Studies,* vol. 13 of *The Collected Works,* The Bollingen Series (Princeton: Princeton University Press, 1968), para. 395.

2. Plowman, *Introduction to the Study of Blake,* p. 93.

Chapter 5 / Courtesy and an Interior Hierarchy of Values

1. Julia de Beausobre, *The Woman Who Couldn't Die* (London: Victor Gollanz, 1948).
2. Leo Tolstoy, *War and Peace,* Book XV, chapter 13.
3. C. S. Lewis, *Essays Presented to Charles Williams* (Oxford: Oxford University Press, 1947), p. x.
4. John Moore, *The Waters Under the Earth* (New York: J. B. Lippencott, 1965), pp. 249–50.

Chapter 6 / The King and the Principles of the Heart

1. J. R. R. Tolkein, *The Lord of the Ring,* vol. 2 (Boston: Houghton Mifflin, 1963), p. 278.
2. Harold Goddard, *The Meaning of Shakespeare,* vol. 1 (Chicago: University of Chicago Press, 1967), p. 141.
3. Taken from the *I Ching or Book of Changes,* trans. C. F. Baynes and R. Wilhelm (New York: Bollingen Foundation, 1966), pp. 199, 242, and 157 respectively.

Chapter 7 / It's of No Consequence: The Joy of the Fool

1. *Highlights of Tarot* (Los Angeles: BOTA, 1931), p. 17.
2. Charles Williams, *The Greater Trumps* (Grand Rapids: Wm. B. Eerdmans, 1976), pp. 73–74.
3. R. H. Blyth, *Zen in English Literature and the Oriental Classics* (Tokyo: Hokuseido Press, 1948), p. 369.
4. William Shakespeare, *A Midsummer Night's Dream,* act 5, sc. 1.
5. T. S. Eliot, *Four Quartets,* part 5, 11. 40–41.
6. Williams, *The Greater Trumps,* p. 196.
7. Goddard, *The Meaning of Shakespeare,* vol. 2, p. 136.
8. Introduction by G. K. Chesterton to Charles Dickens's *Dombey and Son* (New York: E. P. Dutton/Everyman, 1907), p. xv.
9. Ibid.

Chapter 8 / Exchange as the Way of Conscious Love

1. Charles Williams and C. S. Lewis, *Arthurian Torso* (Oxford: Oxford University Press, 1969), p. 141.

2. Charles Williams, *He Came Down from Heaven* (London: Faber and Faber, 1950), p. 85.
3. Ibid., p. 96.
4. Charles Williams, "The Founding of the Company," in *Region of the Summer Stars* (Oxford: Oxford University Press, 1950), p. 37.
5. Williams and Lewis, *Arthurian Torso,* p. 142.
6. Williams, *He Came Down from Heaven,* p. 90.
7. Ibid., p. 97.

Chapter 9 / Inner Relationship and Community in the I Ching

1. The English translation of the *I Ching or Book of Changes* used throughout this chapter was made by Cary E. Baynes from Richard Wilhelm's German translation. (It is published by Princeton University Press, with a foreword by C. G. Jung.) Wilhelm has made beautiful summaries of the commentaries as well as translating the text itself, and his deep understanding of Chinese wisdom has truly opened the meaning of the book for the Western world as no purely academic translation could do.
2. C. G. Jung, *Man and His Symbols* (New York: Doubleday, 1964), p. 221.

Chapter 10 / Pride

1. Laurens van der Post, *Heart of the Hunter* (Harmondsworth, Middlesex, England: Penguin Books, 1965).
2. Helen Waddell, *Peter Abelard* (London: Constable and Co., 1948), pp. 194–201.

Chapter 12 / The Lord's Prayer

1. Simone Weil, *Waiting for God* (New York: Capricorn Books, 1952), p. 222.